ADSTRAT

AN ADVERTISING DECISION SUPPORT SYSTEM

by

Hubert Gatignon & Raymond R. Burke

THE WHARTON SCHOOL · UNIVERSITY OF PENNSYLVANIA

▲ *The Scientific Press*

651 Gateway Boulevard • Suite 1100 • South San Francisco, CA 94080-7014

ADSTRAT: AN ADVERTISING DECISION SUPPORT SYSTEM
by Hubert Gatignon and Raymond R. Burke

Printed in the United States of America

10 9 8 7 6 5 4 3 2

ISBN 0-89426-180-0 with 5¼″ disks
ISBN 0-89426-181-9 with 3.5″ disk

Publisher: The Scientific Press
Text design & production editor: Gene Smith
Cover design by Rogondino & Associates

Cover photo © 1991. Geoff Smyth / ACE / Nawrocki Stock Photo, Inc.

CONTENTS

ADSTRAT

AN ADVERTISING DECISION SUPPORT SYSTEM

PREFACE

The ADSTRAT software package was jointly developed by the authors as a means of providing students of advertising with an integrated set of tools and data for assisting a broad range of advertising management decisions. By making these facilities available in a user-friendly package, ADSTRAT helps students to understand and use scientific techniques for advertising decision making. This software is intended to be a pedagogical tool for the future advertiser, advertising or brand manager, account executive, or marketing researcher. The version of ADSTRAT supplied with this manual provides data sets designed especially for educational purposes. However, all of the analysis modules and the content of this manual are appropriate for any real advertising planning situation. By combining ADSTRAT with data bases from specific industries, advertisers can have a comprehensive system for developing a brand's communication program. A professional version of ADSTRAT is available which provides additional utilities for accessing multiple data banks. A supplemental instruction manual and licensing agreement can be obtained from The Scientific Press.

This manual accompanies the educational version of the ADSTRAT software. The manual should be used as a tutorial and reference. The novelty of the ADSTRAT concept resides in its implementation of research work that has been accomplished previously by a number of individuals. While we have added modules that cannot be found outside of ADSTRAT, our main intent is to encourage the use of a diverse set of analytical tools for advertising decision making. To this end, we have paid particular attention to the user's interaction with the computer software. A number of principles guided the design of the ADSTRAT software:

1. *Minimize the amount of time it takes to learn the operation of the system.* The ADSTRAT software uses a menu bar and template format to capitalize on the user's familiarity with other popular software programs. Therefore, class discussion can focus on the decision-support tools rather than on the operational details of the user interface.

2. *Minimize the effort required for students to read data into the analysis package.* ADSTRAT provides default datasets and options for all analysis tools. Format

statements and variable names are stored with the data and are automatically read into the program when data are accessed.

3. *Permit the ADSTRAT user to switch between views of system input and output with a single keystroke to encourage "what-if" analyses.* The ADSTRAT software shows an entire page of user input or system output at a time, and allows the user to switch between these with a single keystroke.

4. *Group analysis tools by advertising decision rather than by estimation method, data requirements, etc.* This helps students to learn which analysis techniques are appropriate for each decision. In addition, for many of the decisions, we provide a range of analysis tools, from simple to sophisticated. In the ADSTRAT system, the student can start with a simple analysis (e.g., examine advertising to sales ratios, costs per thousand, etc.), discover the limitations, and then move to more advanced tools.

5. *Keep the hardware and software requirements to a minimum.* The system only uses memory as it is needed to conserve space and to allow the program to run on small systems. No other application or software drivers are required to run ADSTRAT. It is not necessary to have a hard disk or color monitor. The ADSTRAT software and data operate as a self contained system.

Most of the modules in ADSTRAT were first developed on main frame computers by a variety of researchers using different packages and programming languages. In particular we benefited from the work of Day *et al.* (1975)[1] who had previously adapted the ADBUDG model of Little (1970)[2] for educational purposes. We also recognize the importance of Little and Lodish's MEDIAC model (1969).[3] We adapted their model and program to the personal computer environment, with only minor changes to their original work. MEDIAC is still conceptually and practically one of the richest media allocation models available. Finally, the expert system for advertising decisions is adapted from the work of Burke *et al.* (1990).[4] Although the software was entirely re-programmed for ADSTRAT, the rules used in the knowledge base are basically the same.

ADSTRAT's contribution is therefore to offer an integrated system where the user can compare different approaches and methodologies using various types of data. The results could not have been achieved without the assistance of talented computer programmers. We would like to thank Paul Reber, without whom ADSTRAT would not have had its versatility and ease of use. Gang Shao and Shenjie Guan also contributed their programming expertise on some of the

---

[1] Day, George, Gerald Eskin, David Montgomery, and Charles Weinberg (1975), *Cases in Computer and Model Assisted Marketing: Planning*, Palo Alto, CA: The Scientific Press.

[2] Little, John D. C. (1970), "Models and Managers: The Concept of a Decision Calculus," *Management Science*, 16 (April), B466–485.

[3] Little, John D. C. and Leonard M. Lodish (1969), "A Media Planning Calculus," *Operations Research*, 17 (January-February), 1–35.

[4] Burke, Raymond R., Arvind Rangaswamy, Jerry Wind, and Jehoshua Eliashberg (1990), "A Knowledge-Based System for Advertising Design," *Marketing Science*, 9 (Summer), pp. 212–229.

modules. Finally, James Mendelsohn compiled media information and assembled the data sets. We acknowledge their help.

As discussed in Chapter 1 of this manual, students using ADSTRAT do not need in-depth knowledge of statistical techniques, quantitative methods, or advertising theories. Indeed, the purpose of this software is to show how these methodologies can be used to improve advertising decision making. It would benefit the students, however, to have a minimum level of familiarity with these topics. In particular, a basic understanding of regression analysis, factor analysis, and cluster analysis would facilitate the comprehension of how these methods can be applied to advertising decisions. Therefore, ADSTRAT is not designed to be used in a first course in marketing. Instead, ADSTRAT will maximally benefit undergraduate or graduate students who have already taken the introductory marketing management and quantitative methods courses. ADSTRAT has been used successfully by the authors in advertising courses, both at the MBA and the undergraduate level, at the Wharton School, University of Pennsylvania. We thank our students who have made helpful suggestions during the system's evolution and testing.

This project was funded in part by a grant from IBM. We thank IBM and the Wharton School for their help in completing this project. The authors contributed equally to this work.

Hubert Gatignon
Raymond R. Burke
August 1990

1

Introduction

The objective of the ADSTRAT software package is to familiarize users with the data and methods that are relevant to the job of advertising management. We attempt to demonstrate that there is a science of advertising and that criteria are available for evaluating the quality of advertising decisions. The software package links the theories and concepts of behavioral and management science with the various areas of advertising planning.

The ADSTRAT package provides background information which characterizes a specific situation faced by an advertising decision maker. The reader is first introduced to the industry in which his or her firm operates (Chapter 2). Five firms compete in this industry with a number of brands. Information on the various brands is available over time. The ADSTRAT system takes the user through the various stages in advertising planning, including situation analysis, setting objectives, budgeting, creative strategy, and media planning. The user's task is to develop an advertising plan for one or several brands with the support of ADSTRAT. The final advertising plan can then be justified in terms of the data analyses.

ADSTRAT was designed as a complement and not a substitute for an advertising management textbook. It is assumed that the textbook discusses the field of advertising and the principles of advertising communication. ADSTRAT goes a step beyond this by enabling users to implement the theories, concepts, and analyses described in the textbook and class discussions in a practical decision-making context.

ADSTRAT includes a data base of background information and computer tools which would typically be available to advertising managers. This constitutes an advertising strategy decision support system. In this chapter, we first explain the concept of a decision support system (DSS), and discuss the motivation for the development and usage of a DSS in advertising management. We then present an overview of the various decisions and methods of analysis provided in ADSTRAT and describe the organization of this manual.

What Is a Decision Support System?

Little (1979)[1] introduced the notion of a *Marketing Decision Support System* as a problem-solving technology consisting of a set of tools designed to enhance marketing decisions. The system includes a bank of data relevant to the problem to be solved, models and theories that enable the manager to understand the relationships among the variables in the data, statistics to relate the model to the data and test the manager's theories and ideas, optimization methods to evaluate the possibility of improving performance, and an interactive user interface. All of these elements must work together to provide a useful decision support system.

It is clear that a DSS does not give "the" answer to the manager's problems. It cannot substitute for the decision maker. Instead, it provides various tools which can be applied to data and managerial judgments. The manager must exercise judgment when using these tools, and then combine the system's output with his or her knowledge and experience to reach effective decisions.

Because of the difficulties associated with data collection and statistical analysis and modeling, the responsibility of quantitative analysis has often been delegated to the management scientist rather than to the manager. This situation is changing. Recent developments in data collection and computer hardware and software systems are helping to overcome these barriers, providing managers with direct access to information systems and analytic tools. Indeed, the user interface of a DSS is typically designed to be extremely easy to use. Managers are now using microcomputers themselves to analyze and interpret marketing data sets.

This presents an extremely important benefit. While the management scientist has technical knowledge about data collection and analysis, the manager has direct experience with the market. If the scientist is left to solve the problem, he or she may neglect this valuable market information. When a DSS is used directly by the manager, he or she can combine personal, qualitative knowledge with quantitative research results. Many of the tools in ADSTRAT provide this facility. For example, the expert system for advertising design integrates managerial judgment about consumers and markets with a knowledge base of past research findings to make recommendations.

Why a DSS in Advertising Management?

Advertising decisions are inherently complex and error-prone because of the tremendous variety of communication options and the large number of consumer and environmental factors determining advertising performance. These decisions are likely to become even more difficult in the future. Due to technological changes, consumers are receiving information faster, so their knowledge, interests, and lifestyles are changing faster. The complexity of the marketplace is also increasing. Marketers have increased the volume of new product introductions, advertising, and promotion activities. In 1988, consumer packaged-goods manufacturers introduced over 10,000 new products, and this number is increasing by about 10% per year.[2]

Within this complex environment, advertisers are forced to make an increasing number of advertising decisions. Many decisions, such as copy design and media planning, are now made at the regional level. Advertisers must also choose between an increasing number of creative options, promotion options, and media options.

Fortunately, technological developments have provided marketers with more detailed information on consumers and markets than ever before. (It is estimated that product managers are supplied with one billion new numbers each week.) There has also been an increase in the amount of published advertising research. Over the last ten years, there have been a number of significant new theoretical and empirical findings. However, the data and theory are hard to use. Much of the advertising knowledge is locked up in textbooks and journal articles, and is not available at the time of advertising decisions. Some advertisers are also concerned that quantitative analyses may inhibit their creative freedom.

The purpose of an advertising decision support system is to allow advertisers to make better use of available information in order to design more effective advertising campaigns. The system should allow advertisers to explore a broader range of alternatives, thus expanding rather than restricting their creativity. It should facilitate the analysis of consumer and market information so that judgments can be based on facts rather than intuition.

Another potential benefit of an advertising decision support system is improved coordination and integration. The system can help to insure a link between market analysis and advertising strategy and tactics. The system combines data from multiple sources with relevant models, analyses, and decision tools. The system helps to provide a rationale for advertising decisions, and can be used to coordinate the activities of the many individuals involved in developing an ad campaign.

The challenge when developing and using an advertising DSS is to address both the quantitative and qualitative aspects of advertising decisions. A deep understanding of consumer emotions and motivations is critical, not just for advertising copy design, but for all aspects of advertising planning. It is the advertiser's responsibility to use all the information available to make the best decisions possible. We attempt to address this in ADSTRAT by providing detailed information on consumer motivations, psychographics, and decision processes, as well as purchase behavior and media habits, and by including computer methods for quantitative and qualitative analyses.

How Does ADSTRAT Relate to Other Teaching Methods?

From a pedagogical point of view, the objectives of an advertising class are to demonstrate how behavioral and management science knowledge and techniques can be applied to advertising decisions. To date, there exist three different tools for teaching advertising management. Traditional textbooks and lectures are the mainstay of advertising instruction. They are an efficient means of communicating information about the advertising field and behavioral science. Unfortunately, textbooks often provide insufficient or inaccessible coverage of quantitative methods. The ADSTRAT system brings data and models to life, allowing students to experiment with the methods to identify their benefits and limitations.

Another pedagogical tool, cases, can provide a context for exploring advertising issues. Yet, students are limited as to the kinds of analyses they can perform on case data. The few advertising cases that are accompanied by computer software tools typically cover only one aspect of advertising planning.

Many advertising courses require students to design an advertising plan or campaign for an existing brand. Students spend a considerable amount of time in the library searching for secondary data, and/or conducting marketing research studies using small and unrepresentative samples. In some cases, there is insufficient time or data available for students to do a complete analysis. The ADSTRAT package solves many of these problems. A substantial database of consumer and market information is readily available. ADSTRAT makes it easy to analyze this information. The system enables students to consider multiple approaches and gain different perspectives on the decision making process.

Organization of the ADSTRAT Manual

The ADSTRAT manual is organized according to the stages in developing an advertising plan. Chapter 2 introduces the reader to the ADSTRAT market and competitive environment and presents a detailed description of the accompanying datasets. The ADSTRAT package includes four types of data commonly available to advertising managers: industry data, panel data, survey data, and media cost and coverage data. Industry and panel data have been generated using the MARKSTRAT[3] market simulation program. When ADSTRAT is used for classroom instruction, instructors will typically assign the various brands to one or more students in the class. Students are then asked to develop advertising campaigns for their brands.

Chapter 3 discusses the process of situation analysis, and describes the ADSTRAT tools for conducting consumer, product, and market analyses. These analyses will reveal a set of problems and opportunities which are the basis for subsequent advertising decisions.

The remaining chapters cover each advertising decision that needs to be made in the course of developing an advertising campaign. Chapter 4 discusses methods for setting a brand's communication objectives. Chapter 5 presents different approaches to the advertising budget decision. Advertising creative strategy and copy design are discussed in Chapter 6. Finally, Chapter 7 is concerned with the selection of communication media and vehicles, and the scheduling of advertising over time.

Each chapter in this manual reviews the conceptual foundations for the methodologies presented, and provides the information necessary for the user to apply these techniques. No special technical knowledge is required for the student to use the software and benefit from this learning experience. If the reader is interested in a general introduction to statistical analysis procedures (such as regression and factor analysis), expert systems, or optimization methods, he or she should consult textbooks in these areas.

As noted earlier, the software has been designed to be easy to use and to require minimal computer training. However, some basic knowledge of personal computers and software is necessary. The Appendix provides instructions on how to load and use the ADSTRAT software package. It serves as a reference guide for the general functions of the software. Each chapter then discusses the specific options available for the corresponding decision modules. Examples are provided with the discussion of each module. The reader should note that the numbers shown in the examples are for illustration purposes only and may not correspond to the actual data supplied with ADSTRAT. We recommend that the reader first *review the Appendix* before proceeding to Chapter 2 so that he or she can interact with the software while reading the manual.

References

1. Little John D. C. (1979), "Decision Support Systems for Marketing Managers," *Journal of Marketing*, 43 (Summer), 9–26.
2. Fannin, Rebecca (1989), "Where Are the New Brands?" *Marketing & Media Decisions*, July, 22–27.
3. Larréché, Jean Claude and Hubert Gatignon (1990), *MARKSTRAT2: A Marketing Strategy Simulation*, Redwood City, CA: The Scientific Press.

2

ADSTRAT Data

Effective advertising campaigns are based on a systematic and detailed analysis of product, market, media, and consumer information. Advertisers obtain this information from a variety of sources. Library research can reveal information on industry and consumer trends. Marketing research companies specialize in measuring consumer characteristics and tracking consumer purchase behavior. Circulation audit and media research companies monitor consumers' exposure to magazines, newspapers, television programs, and other media. Advertisers and their agencies conduct a considerable amount of research in house, especially focus groups and personal interviews, to understand consumers' motivations and decision processes. To enrich the user's educational experience with ADSTRAT, we have attempted to provide a representative cross-section of these various types of information.

The ADSTRAT system provides four different kinds of information: industry, panel, survey, and media data. ADSTRAT's industry dataset includes aggregate product and market data for all of the brands sold in each time period. This type of information is often provided by market research services, trade and business publications, and trade associations to all of the firms competing in an industry. The next two datasets contain information collected from a sample of consumers rather than from the entire population. The first, panel data, is gathered from a group of consumers who have agreed to periodically record their brand perceptions, preferences, and purchase behavior. This information is often purchased by advertisers from syndicated research services and is useful for tracking changes in consumer behavior over time. The second, survey data, is collected by questionnaire or personal interview from a large group of consumers. Surveys are often conducted by advertising agencies (such as DDB Needham Worldwide, N. W. Ayer, and others), survey research companies, and by the advertisers themselves. These surveys typically measure a broad range of consumer characteristics, including attitudes, interests, values, and lifestyles. This

7

information is especially useful for selecting target audiences and designing creative appeals. A fourth dataset provides information on media costs and audience coverage. These data are usually obtained from media representatives or media research companies.

As noted earlier, the MARKSTRAT[1] market simulation program was used to create the industry and panel datasets which accompany ADSTRAT. The survey dataset was developed separately to conform to this environment. In this chapter, we first describe the MARKSTRAT environment and the characteristics of the industry. We then present the four types of ADSTRAT data and discuss the contents of each dataset.

The MARKSTRAT Environment[2]

To understand the industry in which competing firms operate, the reader must be familiar with two general dimensions of the MARKSTRAT environment: (1) the structure of the industry in terms of the products, competition, and market characteristics, and (2) the marketing decisions that each firm can make over time. The discussion which follows concentrates on those aspects which are most relevant to advertising planning decisions.

Competition and Market Structure

In the MARKSTRAT environment (as used in ADSTRAT), five firms compete in a single market with a number of brands. Each firm starts out with a set of brands and has the ability to initiate research and development (R&D) projects to create new brands. If an R&D project is successful, then the sponsoring firm has the option of bringing the new product to market. All new products are introduced with new brand names.

Product Characteristics. The generic products in this industry are consumer durable goods comparable to electronic entertainment products. They are called Sonites. Because these products are durable, each customer will usually purchase only one item over a long period of time. Consequently, there are no issues of repeat purchase, brand loyalty, or brand switching in the data provided with ADSTRAT.

The products are characterized by five physical attributes: (1) weight (in kilograms), (2) design (measured on a relative scale), (3) volume (in cubic decimeters), (4) maximum frequency (in kilohertz), and (5) power (in watts). Not all attributes are equally important to consumers. Different segments have different preferences for these product characteristics, although the preferences are expressed in terms of brand image rather than purely physical characteristics. Consumers' brand evaluations are a function of their perceptions of the brands on three general dimensions, roughly corresponding to three of the five physical characteristics listed above. The first and most important characteristic is the perceived price of the product. Next, people consider the product's power (wattage). Finally, consumers evaluate the product's design (aesthetic value). Although less important than the other dimensions, the product's design helps consumers to differentiate between the various competing brands. The design attribute is measured on a scale from 1 to 10 by expert judges. To form an overall evaluation of each brand, consumers compare the brand's performance on each dimension with their preferences for a certain "ideal level" on each of these dimensions.

Because of the durability of the Sonite product and the importance of the purchase, the consumer decision process tends to follow a "high involvement" hierarchy.[3] Measures of brand awareness, perceptions, preferences, and purchase intentions are, therefore, particularly relevant to the advertising decisions.

Consumer Segments. The consumer market for Sonites can be decomposed into five segments with distinguishable preferences. Segment 1 consists primarily of the "buffs," or experts in the product category. They are innovators and have high standards and requirements in terms of the technical quality of the product. Segment 2 is composed of "singles" who are relatively knowledgeable about the product but somewhat price sensitive. "Professionals" are found mostly in segment 3. They are demanding in terms of product quality and are willing to pay a premium price for that quality. "High earners" constitute segment 4. These individuals are also relatively price insensitive. However, they are not as educated as the professionals, and are not particularly knowledgeable about the product category. They buy the product mostly to enhance their social status. The fifth and last segment covers all consumers who cannot be grouped with any of the other four segments. They have used the product less than consumers in other segments and are considered to be late adopters of this product category. Given that this group is defined as a residual, it is very difficult to characterize the members in terms of demographics or lifestyle.

Although the preferences of the five consumer segments may change over time, the composition of each segment does not. Consequently, the survey data collected in the eighth time period (to be described) also describes consumers during the previous seven periods.

Distribution Structure. Sonites are sold through three different channels of distribution. Each channel carries all brands of Sonites, but the potential number of distributors and the characteristics of each channel are different. Channel 1 is made up of specialty retail stores. These stores provide specialized services to customers, and the bulk of their sales come from Sonites. There are 3,000 such outlets. Electric appliance stores are channel number 2. The 35,000 appliance stores carry Sonite products only as an addition to their main lines of electric appliances. Channel 3 is the 4,000 department stores that exist in the MARKSTRAT world. Department stores sell a broad range of products, including clothing, furniture, housewares, and appliances. The three channels differ in terms of the proportion of the product that they sell and the types of clientele that they attract.

Marketing Mix Decisions

A product's marketing mix has a major impact on advertising strategy. A brand's attributes will influence how the brand is positioned and to whom it is marketed. Its price will affect the advertising budget and the brand image. Its distribution will determine where the brand is advertised, and so on. In this section, we review the four main marketing mix variables, price, sales force, advertising, and product, that characterize brands in the MARKSTRAT environment.

Prices. Each Sonite brand has a recommended retail price. These prices are generally accepted by the distribution channels and are passed on to consumers. As indicated earlier, different consumer segments are more or less sensitive to price differences across brands. A segment's price sensitivity or "elasticity" also depends on the selection of products offered to that segment and on the other marketing mix variables.

Sales Force. The two most important aspects of a firm's sales force are its size and its assignment to the three channels of distribution. Each salesperson carries the entire line of brands produced by his or her company. When a firm changes the number of salespeople it assigns to a particular channel, this is likely to affect the availability or distribution coverage of the firm's brands.

Advertising. Each brand of Sonite is advertised individually. Firms in this industry do not practice umbrella or generic (product category) advertising. However, advertising of specific brands can increase the total market demand for Sonites or affect Sonite demand in one or more segments. Consequently, ADSTRAT users should not neglect the effects of advertising on primary demand.

Advertising can serve a number of communication purposes. It can be used to increase top-of-mind brand awareness and inform consumers about a brand's characteristics. Research has revealed that advertising expenditures are strongly positively related to brand awareness. Advertising can also have a substantial persuasive effect on consumers. Advertising can be used to position or reposition a brand so that the brand's image is more closely aligned with consumers' needs.

In addition, it is clear that advertising plays an important competitive role. One cannot consider a brand's advertising in isolation. Instead, the relative advertising weight or "share of voice" is a better predictor of consumers' purchase behavior than absolute advertising expenditures. Share of voice is the ratio of the brand's advertising expenditures to the total industry spending on advertising.

Products. The ADSTRAT database reports information on all of the Sonite products that were marketed by firms during an eight-year time period. The names of the brands sold during this period are listed in Table 2.1. This Table also lists the periods during which each brand was available. The reader should note that some of the brands were introduced after the first time period and/or were discontinued before the last (eighth) period.

The brands of Sonites are named to facilitate identification of the marketing firm. The second letter of each brand name is a vowel that corresponds to one of the five competing firms. Firm 1 markets all brands that have an "A" as the second letter of the name, such as SAMA. "E" corresponds to firm 2, "I" to firm 3, "O" to firm 4, and "U" to firm 5.

During the eight time periods, each firm has the opportunity to design and market a portfolio of different brands. In response to consumer or market pres-

―――――――――――――――――――――――― **Table 2.1** ――――――――――――――――――――

Names of Brands Marketed During Each Period

Firm	Brand	Period of Availability
1	SAMA	1–8
	SALT	1–8
	SARK	3–8
	SANE	4–8
2	SEMI	1–8
	SELF	1–6*
	SELA	5–7*
	SENE	6–6*
3	SIBI	1–8
	SIRO	1–6*
	SIAA	3–8
4	SONO	1–8
	SOLD	1–8
	SODA	5–6*
5	SULI	1–8
	SUSI	1–8
	SULU	6–8

*Indicates a discontinued brand

sures, companies may change the physical characteristics of each brand over time. Information about brands and their attributes is provided in the industry data set, as described below.

Industry Data

The industry dataset provides two types of performance information for each brand and time period: sales figures (in units and dollar sales) and market share data (based on unit and dollar sales). The dataset also includes information on the values of the marketing mix variables for each competing brand. The data describe each brand's price, advertising expenditures, sales force size (for each channel of distribution), and physical characteristics (i.e., the four P's). Finally, the dataset reports the variable cost of each brand at each time period. The reader should note that this cost is not the actual current production cost, as this information is typically not available for each competitive brand. The reported cost figures reflect the basic cost of production that can be estimated for a given first batch of 100,000 units at the period of introduction of the brand. A list of the variables in the industry dataset is given in Table 2.2.

Panel Data

The panel dataset provides information that, in many ways, complements the data in the industry dataset. Panel data are available at the level of the individual market segment rather than at the total market level. The panel dataset includes

---
Table 2.2

Variables in Industry Level Data Base

Abbreviation	Variable
Period	Period Number
Firm	Firm Number
Brand	Brand Name
Price	Price
Advert	Advertising Expenditures
Char01	Product Characteristic #1: Weight (Kg)
Char02	Product Characteristic #2: Design (Index)
Char03	Product Characteristic #3: Volume (dm^3)
Char04	Product Characteristic #4: Maximum Frequency (khz)
Char05	Product Characteristic #5: Power (W)
Salesmen1	Number of Salesmen—Channel 1
Salesmen2	Number of Salesmen—Channel 2
Salesmen3	Number of Salesmen—Channel 3
Cost	Average Unit Cost of Initial Batch
Dist01	Number of Distributors—Channel 1
Dist02	Number of Distributors—Channel 2
Dist03	Number of Distributors—Channel 3
UnitSales	Total Sales in Units
DolSales	Total Sales in Dollars
UnitShare	Market Share (Based on Units)
DolShare	Market Share (Based on Dollars)
AdShare	Advertising Share (Share of Voice)
RelPrice	Relative Price (Price relative to average market price)

---

information on the size of each segment (in unit sales of Sonites) and the market share for each brand with each segment. The dataset also provides the results of a panel questionnaire with items on advertising communication, brand perceptions, and preferences. Variables include the extent of brand name awareness, segment preferences in terms of the ideal levels of the three most important attributes (price, power, and design), consumers' brand perceptions on the same three dimensions, and brand purchase intentions. Finally, the dataset reports the shopping habits of each segment in the three channels of distribution. A summary of these variables is provided in Table 2.3.

Survey Data

A mail survey of a group of 300 consumers was conducted in the eighth (most recent) time period. The survey collected a variety of consumer information including demographic data, psychographics, information on product purchase behavior, decision processes, and media habits. These data are particularly useful for segmentation analysis, which is an important precursor to selecting a target market, generating copy appeals, and media selection. A list of the variables from the questionnaire and the coding scheme for the items are provided in Tables 2.4 and 2.5 respectively. This information is discussed in more detail in Chapter 3.

--- **Table 2.3** ---

Variables in Panel Data Base

Abbreviation	Variable
Period	Period Number
Segment	Segment Number
SegSize	Segment Size (Unit Sales in Segment)
Ideal01	Ideal Value of Price (for each segment)
Ideal02	Ideal Value of Power (for each segment)
Ideal03	Ideal Value of Design (for each segment)
Brand	Brand Name
Awareness	Percentage of segment aware of the brand
Intent	Purchase Intent (for each brand and segment)
Shop01	Percentage of segment shopping in Channel 1
Shop02	Percentage of segment shopping in Channel 2
Shop03	Percentage of segment shopping in Channel 3
Perc01	Perception of Price (for each brand)
Perc02	Perception of Power (for each brand)
Perc03	Perception of Design (for each brand)
Dev01	Deviation from Ideal Price (for each brand in each segment)
Dev02	Deviation from Ideal Power (for each brand in each segment)
Dev03	Deviation from Ideal Design (for each brand in each segment)
Share	Segment Share (for each brand)

--- **Table 2.4** ---

Survey Questionnaire and Scale Type

Number	Abbreviation	Question	Scale
		DEMOGRAPHICS	
1	Age	Age	continuous
2	Marital	Marital status	categorical
3	Income	Total household income	categorical
4	Education	Education	categorical
5	HHSize	Household size	continuous
6	Occupation	Occupation	categorical
7	Location	Geographic location of household	categorical
		PSYCHOGRAPHICS	
8	TryHairdo	I often try the latest hairdo styles.	likert
9	LatestStyle	I usually have one or more outfits that are of the very latest style.	likert
10	DressSmart	An important part of my life and activities is dressing smartly.	likert
11	BlondsFun	I really do believe that blondes have more fun.	likert*
12	LookDif	I want to look a little different from others.	likert
13	LookAttract	Looking attractive is important in keeping your husband (wife).	likert
14	GrocShop	I like grocery shopping.	likert
15	LikeBaking	I love to bake and frequently do.	likert
16	ClothesFresh	Clothes should be dried in the fresh air and out-of-doors.	likert
17	WashHands	It is very important for people to wash their hands before eating every meal.	likert
18	Sporting	I would rather go to a sporting event than a dance.	likert
19	LikeColors	I like bright, splashy colors.	likert

*likert items are scaled from 1 = Disagree to 7 = Agree

--- Table 2.4 ---

(*continued*)

Number	Abbreviation	Question	Scale
		PSYCHOGRAPHICS (*continued*)	
20	FeelAttract	I like to feel attractive.	likert
21	TooMuchSex	There is too much emphasis on sex today.	likert
22	Social	I do more things socially than do most of my friends.	likert
23	LikeMaid	I would like to have a maid to do the housework.	likert
24	ServDinners	I like to serve unusual dinners.	likert
25	SaveRecipes	I save recipes from newspapers and magazines.	likert
26	LikeKitchen	The kitchen is my favorite room.	likert
27	LoveEat	I love to eat.	likert
28	SpiritualVal	Spiritual values are more important than material things.	likert
29	Mother	If it was good enough for my mother, it's good enough for me.	likert
30	ClassicMusic	Classical music is more interesting than popular music.	likert
31	Children	I try to arrange my home for my children's convenience.	likert
32	Appliances	It is important to have new appliances.	likert
33	CloseFamily	Our family is a close-knit group.	likert
34	LoveFamily	There is a lot of love in our family.	likert
35	TalkChildren	I spend a lot of time with my children talking about their activities, friends, and problems.	likert
36	Exercise	Everyone should take walks, bicycle, garden, or otherwise exercise several times a week	likert
37	LikeMyself	I like what I see when I look in the mirror.	likert
38	CareOfSkin	I take good care of my skin.	likert
39	MedCheckup	You should have a medical checkup at least once a year.	likert
40	EveningHome	I would rather spend a quiet evening at home than go out to a party.	likert
41	TripWorld	I would like to take a trip around the world.	likert
42	Homebody	I am a homebody.	likert
43	LondonParis	I would like to spend a year in London or Paris.	likert
44	Comfort	I furnish my home for comfort, not for style.	likert
45	Ballet	I like ballet.	likert
46	Parties	I like parties where there is lots of music and talk.	likert
47	WomenNtSmoke	Women should not smoke in public.	likert
48	BrightFun	I like things that are bright, fun, and exciting.	likert
49	Seasoning	I am interested in spices and seasoning.	likert
50	ColorTV	If I had to choose, I would rather have a color television set than a new refrigerator.	likert
51	SloppyPeople	Sloppy people feel terrible.	likert
		PURCHASE BEVAVIOR	
52	Smoke	How often do you smoke?	0 to 7
53	Gasoline	How much gasoline do you use?	0 to 7
54	Headache	How much do you use headache remedies?	0 to 7
55	Whiskey	How much do you drink whiskey?	0 to 7
56	Bourbon	How much do you drink bourbon?	0 to 7
57	FastFood	How often do you eat at fast food restaurants?	0 to 7
58	Restaurants	How often do you eat at restaurants with table service?	0 to 7
59	OutForDinner	How often do you go out for dinner?	0 to 7
60	OutForLunch	How often do you go out for lunch?	0 to 7
61	RentVideo	How often do you rent video tapes?	0 to 7
62	Catsup	How often do you use catsup?	0 to 7

--- **Table 2.4** ---

(continued)

Number	Abbreviation	Question	Scale
		PURCHASE DECISION PROCESS	
63	KnowledgeSon	How much do you know about the product category of Sonites?	likert
64	PerceiveDif	How large a difference do you perceive between various brands of Sonites?	likert
65	BrandLoyalty	When purchasing a Sonite, how loyal are you to a particular brand name?	likert
66	CategMotiv	What is your primary reason or motivation for purchasing a Sonite (the product category)?	categorical
67	BrandMotiv	What is your primary reason or motivation for purchasing a particular brand of Sonite?	categorical
68	OwnSonite	Do you currently own a Sonite?	0/1
69	NecessSonite	Do you feel that owning a Sonite is a necessity?	0/1
70	OtherInflnc	If you were to purchase a Sonite, would you make the decision about which brand to purchase by yourself or with the help of others?	categorical
71	DecisionTime	If you were to purchase a Sonite, would you make the decision about which brand to purchase before going to the retail store, or would you wait until you were in the store to decide?	categorical
		MEDIA HABITS	
72	ReadWomen	I read Women's magazines.	0/1
73	ReadHomeServ	I read Home Service magazines.	0/1
74	ReadFashion	I read Fashion magazines.	0/1
75	ReadMenMag	I read Men's magazines.	0/1
76	ReadBusMag	I read Business and Financial magazines.	0/1
77	ReadNewsMag	I read News magazines.	0/1
78	ReadGlMag	I read General magazines.	0/1
79	ReadYouthMag	I read Youth magazines.	0/1
80	ReadNwspaper	I read the newspaper.	0/1
81	WtchDayTV	I watch network television during the day time.	0/1
82	WtchEveTV	I watch network television early evening news.	0/1
83	WtchPrmTV	I watch network television during prime time.	0/1
84	WtchLateTV	I watch network television in the late evening.	0/1
85	WtchWkEndTV	I or my kid(s) watch children's programs on television during the weekend.	0/1
86	WtchCosbyTV	I watch The Cosby Show regularly.	0/1
87	WtchFamTisTV	I watch Family Ties regularly.	0/1
88	WtchCheersTV	I watch Cheers regularly.	0/1
89	WtchMoonTV	I watch Moonlighting regularly.	0/1
90	WtchBossTV	I watch Who's the Boss regularly.	0/1
91	WtchGrwTV	I watch Growing Pains regularly.	0/1
92	WtchMiaVicTV	I watch Miami Vice regularly.	0/1
93	WtchDynasTV	I watch Dynasty regularly.	0/1
94	WtchGoldGTV	I watch Golden Girls regularly.	0/1
95	WtchBowlTV	I watch the Superbowl each year.	0/1

Media Data

The media dataset includes information on the ad insertion costs and audience sizes for a large selection of advertising media and vehicles.[4] The data are not

Table 2.5

Coding of Variables

Variable	Category	Code
Question #2 Marital Status	Married	1
	Widowed	2
	Divorced	3
	Separated	4
	Single	5
Question #3: Household Income	Less than $4,000	1
	$4,000 to $5,999	2
	$6,000 to $7,999	3
	$8,000 to $9,999	4
	$10,000 to $11,999	5
	$12,000 to $14,999	6
	$15,000 to $17,499	7
	$17,500 to $19,999	8
	$20,000 to $24,999	9
	$25,000 to $29,999	10
	$30,000 to $49,999	11
	$50,000 and over	12
Question #4: Education Level	Did not attend school	1
	Went to elementary or grammar school	2
	Went to high school or trade school for less than four years	3
	Graduated from high school or trade school	4
	Some college, jr. college, or technical school	5
	Graduated from college	6
	Have post-graduate degree	7
Question #6: Occupation	Professional workers	1
	Managers & administrators, except farm	2
	Clerical workers	3
	Sales workers	4
	Craftsmen	5
	Operatives, except transport	6
	Transport equipment operators	7
	Laborers, except farm	8
	Farmers, farm managers, laborers & foremen	9
	Service & private household workers	0
Question #7 Location	New York	1
	Los Angeles	2
	Chicago	3
	Philadelphia	4
	San Francisco	5
	Boston	6

specific to the Sonite product category or brands, but instead represent the actual costs and total audience coverage of these alternatives. The figures are current as of the date of publication of this manual. The data set does not contain information on the duplication or "external overlap" of audiences across media vehicles. Table 2.6 lists the media vehicles contained in the media database along with the abbre-

---

Table 2.5

(continued)

Variable	Category	Code
Question #7 *(continued)*	Detroit	7
	Dallas	8
	Washington	9
	Houston	10
	Cleveland	11
	Atlanta	12
	Pittsburgh	13
	Miami	14
	Minneapolis-St. Paul	15
	Seattle-Tacoma	16
	Tampa-St. Petersburg	17
	St. Louis	18
	Denver	19
	Sacramento-Stockton	20
Question #66 Category Purchase Motivation	To remove a problem	1
	To avoid a problem	2
	To replace another Sonite	3
	For sensory stimulation	4
	For intellectual stimulation	5
	For social approval	6
	To enhance my self esteem	7
Question #67 Brand Purchase Motivation	To remove a problem	1
	To avoid a problem	2
	Because of dissatisfaction with my current brand	3
	For sensory stimulation	4
	For intellectual stimulation	5
	For social approval	6
	To enhance my self esteem	7
Question #70 Decision Making	By myself (individually)	1
	With the help of others (as a group)	2
Question #71 Decision Timing	Before going to the store	1
	In the store	2

OTHER VARIABLES:

Questions	Scale
8 to 51 63 to 65	Disagree 1 2 3 4 5 6 7 Agree
52 to 62	Never/None 0 1 2 3 4 5 6 7 Very Often/A Lot
68 & 69 72 to 95	0 = No 1 = Yes

---

viated names which appear in the ADSTRAT analysis modules.[5] The cost figures stored in the database represent, in the case of magazines, the cost of placing one full-page, black and white (BW) or full color (4C), advertisement; in the case of newspapers, the cost of running one quarter-page black and white advertisement; and, in the case of television, the cost of showing a 30 second TV commercial.

Table 2.6

Media Options

Media Option Abbreviation	Media Option Name	Frequency of Issue
WOMEN'S MAGAZINES:		
Cosmopoltn	Cosmopolitan	Monthly
GoodHskpng	Good Housekeeping	Monthly
LadiesHJrn	Ladies' Home Journal	Monthly
McCalls	McCall's	Monthly
ParentMgzn	Parents Magazine	Monthly
Redbook	Redbook	Monthly
Seventeen	Seventeen	Monthly
TrueStory	True Story	Monthly
WomansDay	Woman's Day	Monthly
WomansWld	Woman's World	Monthly
HOME SERVICE MAGAZINES:		
BetHomGdns	Better Homes & Garden	Monthly
CountryHom	Country Home	Monthly
CountryLiv	Country Living	Monthly
FamHndyman	Family Handyman	Monthly
Home	Home	Monthly
HouseBtfl	House Beautiful	Monthly
MtrpltnHom	Metropolitan Home	Monthly
1001Homlds	1001 Home Ideas	Monthly
SouthrnLiv	Southern Living	Monthly
Sunset	Sunset	Monthly
FASHION MAGAZINES:		
Bazaar	Bazaar	Monthly
Elle	Elle	Monthly
Glamour	Glamour	Monthly
Madmoisell	Mademoiselle	Monthly
Vogue	Vogue	Monthly
MEN'S MAGAZINES:		
Playboy	Playboy	Monthly
Penthouse	Penthouse	Monthly
Field&Strm	Field & Stream	Monthly
Esquire	Esquire	Monthly
GQ	Gentlemen's Quarterly	Monthly
BUSINESS & FINANCIAL MAGAZINES:		
BusinessWk	Business Week	Weekly
Forbes	Forbes	Biweekly
Fortune	Fortune	27 per Year
Inc	Inc.	Monthly
IndustryWk	Industry Week	Biweekly
NatsBsnss	Nation's Business	Monthly
RealEstTod	Real Estate Today	9 per Year
Savvy	Savvy	Monthly

Table 2.6

(continued)

Media Option Abbreviation	Media Option Name	Frequency of Issue
NEWS MAGAZINES:		
Jet	Jet	Weekly
Newsweek	Newsweek	Weekly
People	People	Weekly
SportsIll	Sports Illustrated	Weekly
SportngNws	Sporting News	Weekly
Time	Time	Weekly
TVGuide	TVGuide	Weekly
Us	Us	Biweekly
USNws&Wld	U.S. News & World Report	Weekly
GENERAL MAGAZINES:		
ChngngTime	Changing Times	Monthly
Life	Life	Monthly
ModMaturity	Modern Maturity	Monthly
Money	Money	Monthly
NatlEnq	National Enquirer	Weekly
NatlGeogr	National Geographic	Monthly
ReadersDig	Reader's Digest	Monthly
Smithsnian	Smithsonian	Monthly
TheStar	The Star	Weekly
Yankee	Yankee	Monthly
YOUTH MAGAZINES:		
BoysLife	Boy's Life	Monthly
Careers	Careers	3 per Year
FastTimes	Fast Times	9 per year
JrScholast	Junior Scholastic	Biweekly
SesameSt	Sesame Street	10 per Year
NEWSPAPERS:		
NYDailyNews	New York Daily News	Daily
LATimes	Los Angeles Times	Daily
NYTimes	New York Times	Daily
NYPost	New York Post	Daily
PhilaInqr	Philadelphia Inquirer	Daily
WashPost	Washington Post	Daily
ChicagoTrib	Chicago Tribune	Daily
SanFranChron	San Francisco Chronicle	Daily
DetroitNews	Detroit News	Daily
NETWORK TELEVISION		
NatnlDaytmTV	National Network Daytime Programs	
NatEarlyNsTV	National Network Early News	
NatPrimeTmTV	National Network Prime Time Programs	
NatLateEveTV	National Network Late Evening Programs	
NatWkndKidTV	National Network Weekend Children's Programs	

Table 2.6

(continued)

Media Option Abbreviation	Media Option Name	Frequency of Program
MAJOR TELEVISION SHOWS:		
CosbyShowTV	Cosby Show	Weekly
FamilyTiesTV	Family Ties	Weekly
CheersTV	Cheers	Weekly
MoonlghtngTV	Moonlighting	Weekly
WhosTheBssTV	Who's the Boss	Weekly
NightCourtTV	Night Court	Weekly
GrowingPnsTV	Growing Pains	Weekly
MiamiViceTV	Miami Vice	Weekly
DynastyTV	Dynasty	Weekly
GoldenGrlsTV	Golden Girls	Weekly
SuperBowlTV	Super Bowl	Once/Year
SPOT TELEVISION:		
NewYorkTV	New York	
LsAnglsTV	Los Angeles	
ChicagoTV	Chicago	
PhilaTV	Philadelphia	
SanFranTV	San Francisco	
BostonTV	Boston	
DetroitTV	Detroit	
DallasTV	Dallas	
WashingTV	Washington	
HoustonTV	Houston	
ClvlndTV	Cleveland	
AtlantaTV	Atlanta	
MinnStPTV	Minneapolis-St. Paul	
TampaStPTV	Tampa-St. Petersburg	
SttlTacTV	Seattle-Tacoma	
MiamiTV	Miami	
PittbrgTV	Pittsburgh	
StLouisTV	St. Louis	
DenverTV	Denver	
SacStktn	Sacramento-Stockton	

References

1. MARKSTRAT is a Registered Trademark of STRAT*X.
2. This section is adapted from Gatignon, Hubert (1987), "Strategic Studies in MARKSTRAT," *Journal of Business Research*, 15, 6 (December), and from Larréché, Jean Claude and Hubert Gatignon (1990), *opus cited*.
3. Lavidge, Robert J. and Gary A. Steiner (1961), "A Model for Predictive Measurements of Advertising Effectiveness," *Journal of Marketing*, 25, October, 59–62.
4. Data on audience sizes and costs are consistent with data from *Simmons 1988 Study of Media and Markets*, New York: Simmons Market Research Bureau, Inc. and from publications of the Standard Rate & Data Service, Wilmett, IL.
5. We followed the categories provided in Charles H. Patti and Charles F. Frazer (1988), *Advertising: A Decision-Making Approach*, Chicago, Il: The Dryden Press.

3

Situation Analysis

The first step in developing an advertising plan consists of gathering, reviewing, and analyzing information about the product, consumers, and the marketing environment. This "situation analysis" allows the advertiser to identify the problems and opportunities associated with marketing the product. It provides the foundation for all subsequent advertising decisions. In this chapter, we discuss the three main dimensions of situation analysis (product, market, and consumer analysis), and describe the corresponding ADSTRAT tools for displaying and interpreting the information contained in the industry, panel, and survey databases.

Product Analysis

Advertising should be based on a thorough knowledge of the product. Ideally, product knowledge is obtained from a number of sources, including product use, visiting the factory where the product is made, talking with product designers and engineers, and interacting with salespeople, wholesalers, and retailers. While direct interaction with the product is not possible in the Sonite industry, the ADSTRAT package provides a considerable amount of product information. The previous chapter described the Sonite product and its general attributes. The ADSTRAT user can study the benefits and liabilities of individual brands by applying the system's trend analysis module to the industry and panel datasets. Product analysis should include an examination of the brand's pricing, advertising, salesforce, and distribution, as well as its physical characteristics.

Market Analysis

Advertisers ask the same questions about competitors' products as they do about their own brands. This market analysis is the second major dimension of situation analysis. The relative strengths and weaknesses of a brand are revealed by comparing it with other products in the industry. Advertisers also study changes in brand sales and market share over time to understand the evolution of the market. This trend analysis is especially useful when applied to the sales behavior and preferences of individual consumer segments (panel data). The patterns in the data provide information on consumers' product demand and competition, and can guide the development of a communication strategy and the allocation of resources across brands and market segments.

Another useful tool for market analysis is perceptual mapping, which displays consumers' perceptions of the attributes of competing brands along with consumers' ideal attribute levels. ADSTRAT's perceptual mapping module is discussed in the next chapter in the context of brand positioning decisions.

Consumer Analysis

The third, and perhaps most critical aspect of situation analysis is consumer analysis. Before developing an ad campaign, advertisers must know whom they are targeting and what message is likely to motivate potential buyers. Consumer research investigates a large variety of customers' attributes and behavior, including their demographic and psychographic characteristics, product and brand purchase motivations, brand awareness, perceptions, purchase intentions, and purchase behavior, media habits, the decision making unit, and the purchase decision process. This information is provided in ADSTRAT's survey and panel datasets.

Advertisers often characterize the target audience(s) in demographic terms. Demographics are the statistical representation of consumers' social and economic characteristics, and include such variables as age, sex, income, education, and occupation. They are a popular means of describing consumers because they are relatively easy to measure and the same demographic categories can be applied to all individuals.

Demographic variables are strongly related to almost all product purchase decisions. However, they do not reveal why people buy. To develop a better understanding of consumers' motivations and interests, advertisers conduct focus groups, depth interviews, and psychographic surveys. Psychographics refer to the psychological variables that shape consumer behavior. They reflect consumers' activities, interests, opinions, needs, values, and personality traits. When taken together, they can be used to develop advertisements that attract people's attention, touch their emotions, and portray a brand's benefits in a compelling way.

ADSTRAT provides a number of options for analyzing and displaying the demographic, psychographic, and other consumer information in its database. The "Describe" option (factor analysis) summarizes the information contained in a large number of questions by reducing the data to a few general dimensions which discriminate between individuals. The "Classify" option (cluster analysis) clusters the diverse group of survey respondents into a distinct set of categories or market segments. The "Tabulate" and "Regress" options (crosstabulation and regression analysis) provide two means of profiling consumer characteristics. The decision about which option to use depends on the nature of the relationships being analyzed. Crosstabulations can be used to compute the proportion of consumers who possess a given level of an attribute, or to explore the interdependence of two attributes (for example, the relationship between marital status and Sonite ownership). Regression analysis enables the user to investigate the strength of relationships between customers' characteristics and their purchase behavior.

In summary, the situation analysis modules provide a preliminary evaluation of the problems and opportunities in the marketplace. Many of the results will serve as quantitative and qualitative input to subsequent advertising decisions. The decision maker may therefore need to return to the situation analysis modules at later stages in the advertising planning process. All of the modules described in this chapter are accessed through the "Situation" submenu option.

Trend Analysis

Trend analysis is the study of a variable's behavior over time. One way to analyze trends is to plot the value of a variable as a function of time and examine the shape of the relationship. The purpose of trend analysis is to enable the decision maker to assess the present situation and to anticipate what is going to happen in the future. These predictions are based on the assumption that many of the changes in marketing variables (e.g., product sales, advertising expenditures) are due to relatively stable environmental factors that will continue to have an effect in the future (e.g., population growth, inflation). However, there is no guarantee that a past trend will continue in subsequent periods.

Many of the temporal patterns in marketing activities and consumer behavior can have considerable strategic importance. For example, changes in a market segment's demand for a product over time can indicate the product's life cycle stage. This information will have a major impact on the selection of marketing and advertising objectives. Changes in consumer preferences may also indicate the need to reposition a brand in order to remain competitive.

By comparing trends for a number of variables, the user can identify the reasons for a brand's favorable or mediocre performance, and rule out other, inconsistent explanations.[1] For example, a brand's sales may increase, despite consumers' low awareness of the brand, because of a growing number of distributors. Alternatively, a brand may lose share in a segment, not because of its own actions, but because of the increasing marketing efforts of its competitors. The user can study these issues by plotting the advertising, pricing, sales, and other characteristics of competing brands over time.

Selecting the Trend Option

The trend analysis module is accessed by selecting "Module" from the main menu, and then selecting "Situation" and "Trend." The system displays the first page of the trend analysis input template, which lists criteria for case selection. The following page lists the variable names in the industry and panel datasets. The user can scroll through the template pages by pressing the "Page Up" and "Page Down" keys on the computer's cursor control pad. To select cases and variables for analysis, the user should select "Edit" from the main menu, and the cursor will move to the template area (edit mode).

Selecting Cases

The first screen of the trend analysis option asks the user to select the cases from the industry and panel datasets to be included in the analysis (see Figure 3.1). The user first enters the period range to be plotted. The default values are the entire range of periods (one through eight) covered by the data base. In general,

—————————— Figure 3.1 ——————————

Case Selection for Trend Analysis Option

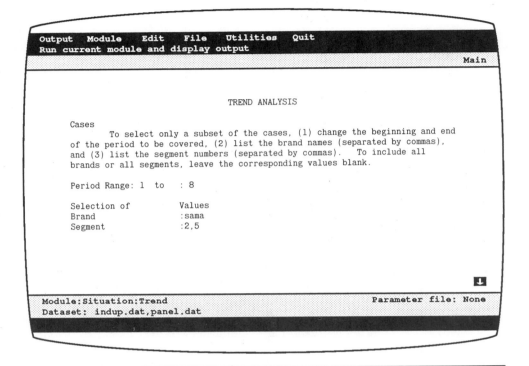

```
Output   Module   Edit   File   Utilities   Quit
Run current module and display output
                                                            Main


                          TREND ANALYSIS

     Cases
              To select only a subset of the cases, (1) change the beginning and end
     of the period to be covered, (2) list the brand names (separated by commas),
     and (3) list the segment numbers (separated by commas).   To include all
     brands or all segments, leave the corresponding values blank.

     Period Range: 1  to   : 8

     Selection of        Values
     Brand               :sama
     Segment             :2,5




                                                                      ⬇

     Module:Situation:Trend                    Parameter file: None
     Dataset: indup.dat,panel.dat
```

users will select the entire eight-year time period so that trends in the data will be most apparent. If a shorter time period is desired, the user can enter the starting period and the final period to be covered by the plot. To create a purely cross-sectional plot, the user can select a single period by entering the same number as the starting and ending period.[2]

ADSTRAT also allows the user to select the specific brands to include in the analysis. If the user does not enter a brand name in the corresponding template field, then the system will plot the data for all of the brands available in the market during the selected time period. However, this comprehensive analysis can obscure the important relationships in the data. Some brands may not be competing for the market segment of interest, and their data are therefore irrelevant. Also, when ADSTRAT plots data for a large number of brands and market segments, many of the data points overlap, and the resulting plot becomes difficult to interpret. It is therefore desirable to include only the relevant brands and periods in the analysis. These brands are selected by typing their respective names, separated by commas, in the corresponding template field. In the example shown in Figure 3.1, the user has requested information on only one brand (SAMA).

Figure 3.2

Selection of a Variable for Trend Option

```
Output   Module    Edit    File    Utilities   Quit
Run current module and display output
                                                              Main
                                                                ⬆
     Check off one variable for analysis from the lists below.

     Industry level variables
          Period:_           Firm:_          Brand:_          Price:_
          Advert:_          Char01:_         Char02:_         Char03:_
          Char04:_          Char05:_       Salesmen1:_      Salesmen2:_
        Salesmen3:_           Cost:_         Dist01:_         Dist02:_
          Dist03:_        UnitSales:_       DolSales:_      UnitShare:_
         DolShare:_         AdShare:_       RelPrice:_

     Segment level variables
          Period:_         Segment:_         SegSize:_        Ideal01:_
         Ideal02:_         Ideal03:_          Brand:_       Awareness:_
          Intent:_          Shop01:_         Shop02:_         Shop03:_
          Perc01:_          Perc02:_         Perc03:_          Share:x


   Module:Situation:Trend
   Dataset: indup.dat,panel.dat                    Parameter file: None
```

If the user is analyzing data obtained from the panel of consumers, then he or she can also select the specific segments to be used in the trend analysis.[3] If no segment numbers are entered in the template field, then, by default, the system plots information for all of the segments. If, however, the user desires to plot only the values of selected segments, then he or she must enter the segment numbers, separated by commas, in the corresponding template field. Figure 3.1 shows an example where data for segments 2 and 5 are requested. Once again, it should be noted that plotting data for multiple segments on the same graph can result in a crowded plot. Therefore, the user should include only those segments which are relevant to the brand.

Selecting a Variable

The trend analysis module can be used to examine the values of any of the variables in the industry and panel datasets. The second screen of the trend analysis template lists the dataset variables, as shown in Figure 3.2. While in edit mode, the user can select a variable by moving the cursor to a check box and pressing the "space bar." Only a single variable should be checked at a time. In

—————————————— Figure 3.3 ——————————————

Example Output of Trend Analysis Option (Screen #1)

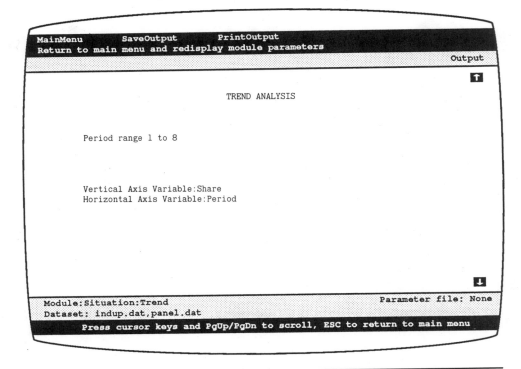

Figure 3.2, market share has been checked off, and will be plotted. The first group of variables, labeled "Industry level variables," come from the industry dataset and are aggregated across all segments. The second block of variables, labeled "Segment level variables," are read from the panel dataset and assume different values for each segment. The reader should refer back to Chapter 2 for a detailed description of the industry and panel dataset variables (Tables 2.2 and 2.3, respectively). To plot the selected variable, the user should "Escape" from edit mode, and then select the "Output" option.

The Trend Analysis Output

Examples of the output displayed by the trend analysis module appear in Figures 3.3 to 3.5. The first screen (Figure 3.3) provides a basic description of the plot, indicating the periods covered and the variables plotted. In this example, the time period appears on the horizontal axis and the market share variable appears on the vertical axis. The second screen (Figure 3.4) shows the plot of market share over time. The third screen (Figure 3.5) provides a legend for the plotted points. The labeling system uses a capital letter for the brand name, followed (in the case of panel dataset variables) by a number corresponding to the segment

— Figure 3.4 —

Example Output of Trend Analysis Option (Screen #2)

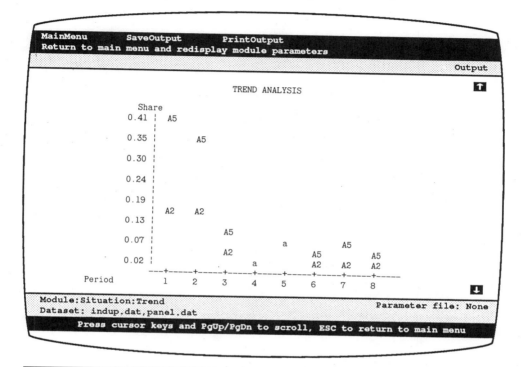

number (1 to 5). Therefore A2 indicates a point corresponding to the share of brand SAMA in market segment 2. If multiple points overlap on the plot, then the system uses lowercase letters to represent the combination of values. For example, as shown in Figure 3.4, SAMA has the same market share in segments 2 and 5 for periods 4 and 5. In Figure 3.5, the label "a" is defined as representing the market shares of brand SAMA in segments 2 and 5.

Summary

In this section, we have discussed a general type of analysis which helps advertisers to understand the dynamics of the marketplace. Although simple, this analysis of trends can reveal the market and competitive factors which determine a brand's success or failure and can help to identify future opportunities for the brand.

Describe Consumers: Psychographics and Factor Analysis

When we analyze a consumer questionnaire, we often observe that many of the items are closely related to each other. Groups of items seem to represent

—————————————————— **Figure 3.5** ——————————————————

Example Output of Trend Analysis Option (Screen #3)

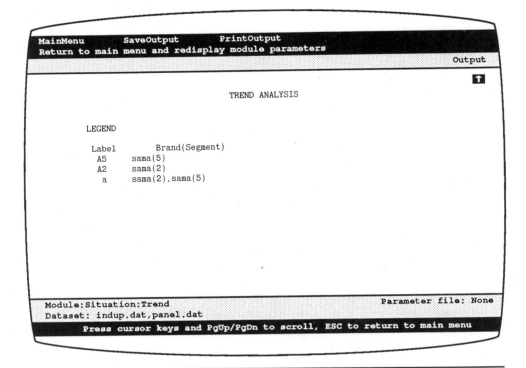

certain underlying dimensions. For example, in the consumer survey which accompanies ADSTRAT (Table 2.4), the 95 questions do not describe 95 independent customer characteristics. Instead, they reflect a smaller set of personality traits, values, habits, and lifestyles. The goal of factor analysis is to "explain" the intercorrelations between observed variables by deriving a reduced set of factors that capture all of the essential, common information in the original set of questions.[4]

Factor analysis has a long tradition in psychology. Spearman[5] factor analyzed various measures of mental ability in order to establish the basic dimensions of human intelligence. Thurstone[6] applied factor analysis to perceptual variables and attitudes, while R. B. Cattell[7] used it to determine human personality traits. In the same spirit, advertisers apply factor analysis to psychographic data to identify the intervening variables that affect consumer behavior.

Selecting the Describe Option

The factor analysis module is accessed by selecting "Module" from the main menu, and then selecting "Situation" and "Describe." The system displays the factor analysis input template, which lists the criterion value for retaining factors

---
Figure 3.6

Selection of Variables for Factor Analysis

```
Output   Module   Edit   File   Utilities   Quit
Run current module and display output
                                                          Main

                 DESCRIBE CONSUMERS -- PSYCHOGRAPHICS
                         AND FACTOR ANALYSIS

     Minimum variance for retaining factor:    1.00

     Check off variables to be included in the analysis

              Age:x      TryHairdo:x     LatestStyle:x      DressSmart:x
           RdFashn:x     BlondsFun:x        LookDif:x      LookAttract:x
           GrocShp:x     LikeBaking:x    ClothesFresh:x      WashHands:x
          Sporting:_     LikeColors:_     FeelAttract:_     TooMuchSex:_
            Social:_       LikeMaid:_      ServDinners:_     SaveRecipes:_
        LikeKitchen:_       LoveEat:_     SpiritualVal:_         Mother:_
        ClassicMusic:_     Children:_       Appliances:_     CloseFamily:_
         LoveFamily:_    TalkChildren:_      Exercise:_      LikeMyself:_
          CareOfSkin:_    MedCheckup:_     EveningHome:_       TripWorld:_
           Homebody:_    LondonParis:_        Comfort:_          Ballet:_
            Parties:_    WomenNtSmoke:_      BrightFun:_       Seasoning:_
            ColorTV:_    SloppyPeople:_

  Module:Situation:Describe                    Parameter file: None
  Dataset: survey.dat
```

and the continuous variables in the survey dataset. To identify variables for analysis, the user should select "Edit" from the main menu. The cursor will move to the template area (edit mode).

Selecting the Minimum Variance Criterion

A primary purpose of factor analysis is to reduce the dataset from a large number of variables to a small set of factors. The user can control the number of factors generated by ADSTRAT by specifying the minimum variance that must be explained by a factor (also called the minimum "eigenvalue" or "characteristic root"). The minimum variance criterion is usually set to one so that each factor accounts for at least as much variance as one of the original variables in the dataset.[8] This is the default value in the factor analysis template. By setting a higher minimum variance criterion, the user can reduce the number of factors. Setting a lower minimum variance will increase the number of factors.

Another technique for setting the minimum variance criterion is called the "scree test."[9] It entails plotting the variance explained by each sequential factor (see ahead, Figure 3.8). The user looks for an "elbow" in the curve; a point at which additional factors do not capture much additional variance. The minimum

─────────────────────────── Figure 3.7 ───────────────────────────

Example Output of Factor Analysis (Screen #1)

```
 MainMenu        SaveOutput        PrintOutput
 Return to main menu and redisplay module parameters
                                                              Output

                    DESCRIBE CONSUMERS -- PSYCHOGRAPHICS
                           AND FACTOR ANALYSIS


        Initial Factor Pattern

                     Factor 1 Factor 2 Factor 3
               Age    -0.178   -0.507   -0.007
          TryHairdo    0.969   -0.057    0.039
         LatestStyle   0.968   -0.021    0.067
         DressSmart    0.968   -0.028    0.043
            RdFashn    0.970   -0.042    0.035
          BlondsFun   -0.023   -0.107   -0.067
            LookDif    0.973   -0.015    0.063
         LookAttract   0.964   -0.018    0.059
            GrocShp   -0.046    0.821    0.502
         LikeBaking   -0.052    0.821    0.493
        ClothesFresh  -0.166   -0.518    0.792
          WashHands   -0.150   -0.515    0.796
                                                               ⬇

 Module:Situation:Describe                    Parameter file: None
 Dataset: survey.dat
       Press cursor keys and PgUp/PgDn to scroll, ESC to return to main menu
```

variance criterion is set at this elbow value to eliminate the remaining factors.

Selecting Variables

The factor analysis template lists the continuous variables from the survey dataset, as shown in Figure 3.6. While in edit mode, the user can select a variable by moving the cursor to a check box and pressing the "space bar." The user can select any number of variables, and is limited only by the memory capacity of the personal computer.[10] In Figure 3.6, the first twelve variables are checked off. To factor analyze the selected variables, the user should "Escape" from edit mode, and then select the "Output" option.

The Factor Analysis Procedure and Output

ADSTRAT first performs classical or "common" factor analysis, factoring a reduced intercorrelation matrix with the principal axes method.[11] The principal axes solution locates the first factor so as to maximize the percent of explained variance, and locates each subsequent, orthogonal factor to explain the maximum residual variance. The results are displayed as the Initial Factor Pattern matrix (Figure 3.7).

--- **Figure 3.8** ---

Example Output of Factor Analysis (Screen #2)

```
MainMenu        SaveOutput         PrintOutput
Return to main menu and redisplay module parameters

                                                                    Output

                                                                      ⬆

    Number of significant factors: 3

    Variance Explained By Each Unrotated Factor

                Variance  Cumulative  Percentage   Cumulative
                Explained  Variance    Explained   Percentage
    Factor  1    5.719      5.719        60.1         60.1
    Factor  2    2.157      7.876        22.7         82.8
    Factor  3    1.777      9.653        18.7        101.5
    Factor  4    0.069      9.722         0.7        102.2
    Factor  5   -0.004      9.718        -0.1        102.1
    Factor  6   -0.007      9.711        -0.1        102.0
    Factor  7   -0.009      9.702        -0.2        101.8
    Factor  8   -0.012      9.690        -0.2        101.6
    Factor  9   -0.017      9.673        -0.3        101.3
    Factor10   -0.039      9.634        -0.3        101.0
    Factor11   -0.051      9.583        -0.5        100.5
    Factor12   -0.061      9.522        -0.5        100.0

                                                                      ⬇

Module:Situation:Describe                       Parameter file: None
Dataset: survey.dat
       Press cursor keys and PgUp/PgDn to scroll, ESC to return to main menu
```

The values (or loadings) in the Factor Pattern Matrix represent the correlations between the derived factors and the original variables. Correlation coefficients indicate the degree of linear relationship between two variables. They customarily range from −1.00 (indicating a perfect negative relationship) through 0.00 (no relationship) to 1.00 (a perfect positive relationship). The sum of the squared loadings for a factor reflect the variance accounted for by that factor. The variance and percent of variance explained by each factor are shown on the second screen (Figure 3.8).

These initial factor locations are mathematically convenient but often have little psychological meaning. For example, the first factor is usually a general factor which has moderately high positive and negative correlations with all of the variables. We would prefer, instead, for each factor to be represented by a small and distinct set of the original variables. Therefore, ADSTRAT transforms this factor matrix to a more meaningful solution using an orthogonal varimax rotation.[12] The varimax rotation makes it easier to interpret the results of the factor analysis by transforming the factor loadings to values close to one or zero, and spreading the variance more evenly across the factors. The results of this transformation are displayed in the Rotated Factor Pattern matrix, as shown in Figure 3.9.[13] The variance accounted for by each rotated factor appears on the following screen (Figure 3.10).

Figure 3.9

Example Output of Factor Analysis (Screen #3)

```
MainMenu        SaveOutput        PrintOutput
Return to main menu and redisplay module parameters
                                                              Output
                                                                 ⬆

       Rotated Factor Pattern

                    Factor 1 Factor 2 Factor 3
             Age    -0.135   -0.444    0.270
        TryHairdo    0.971    0.002   -0.045
       LatestStyle   0.969    0.047   -0.040
       DressSmart    0.968    0.029   -0.057
          RdFashn    0.970    0.013   -0.056
        BlondsFun   -0.019   -0.127   -0.001
          LookDif    0.972    0.050   -0.047
       LookAttract   0.964    0.045   -0.047
          GrocShp   -0.075    0.960    0.019
       LikeBaking   -0.082    0.956    0.012
      ClothesFresh  -0.058   -0.044    0.958
        WashHands   -0.043   -0.039    0.958

                                                                 ⬇

Module:Situation:Describe                    Parameter file: None
Dataset: survey.dat
    Press cursor keys and PgUp/PgDn to scroll, ESC to return to main menu
```

The interpretation and naming of factors is the responsibility of the user. The meaning of each factor is inferred from the set of original variables with which it is most highly correlated. For example, in Figure 3.9, the second factor (Factor 2) is closely related to the variables GrocShop ("I like grocery shopping") and LikeBaking ("I love to bake and frequently do"). One might hypothesize that the underlying construct being measured is the consumer's interest in food and its preparation.

The ADSTRAT program automatically creates a set of factor scores for each respondent in the dataset corresponding to the estimated scores of respondents on the rotated factors. The factor score variables are labeled FACTOR01 to FACTOR0N, where N is the number of factors exceeding the minimum variance criterion. These variables are automatically saved to disk and become available for use in other situation analysis modules. When the user exits the ADSTRAT program, the factor scores are automatically deleted.

Classify Consumers: Cluster Analysis

Very few products, brands, media, and advertisements appeal to everyone. Dif-

──────────── Figure 3.10 ────────────

Example Output of Factor Analysis (Screen #4)

```
MainMenu        SaveOutput        PrintOutput
Return to main menu and redisplay module parameters
                                                              Output
                                                                 ⬆

     Variance Explained By Each Rotated Factor

               Variance  Cumulative   Percentage   Cumulative
               Explained Variance     Explained    Percentage
     Factor 1    5.669     5.669         58.7          58.7
     Factor 2    2.061     7.730         21.3          80.1
     Factor 3    1.923     9.653         19.9         100.0




     Module:Situation:Describe                 Parameter file: None
     Dataset: survey.dat
     Press cursor keys and PgUp/PgDn to scroll, ESC to return to main menu
```

ferent consumers have different characteristics, needs, and wants. Therefore, marketers typically break the large and heterogeneous population of consumers into a more easily understood set of market segments. Each segment should consist of a group of current or potential product users who respond similarly to elements of the marketing mix. A variety of different consumer attributes can be used to segment the population, including demographics, psychographics, benefits desired, and brand purchase behavior. From these segments, the marketer selects one or more target segments which are the focus of the marketing and advertising program. Advertising is designed to speak directly to the specific needs and wants of the target segments.

As discussed in Chapter 1, the management of the various Sonite companies has grouped customers into five adhoc segments. This segment information is stored in the panel dataset, and can be used to evaluate changes in segment preferences and purchase behavior over time (see the section on trend analysis). Cluster analysis provides another means for segmentation, which is based on an empirical analysis of the similarities of consumers.[14] The purpose of cluster analysis is to classify observations into a distinct set of homogeneous categories. It is typically used to identify persons with similar preferences and buying habits.

--- **Figure 3.11** ---

Selection of Variables for Cluster Analysis

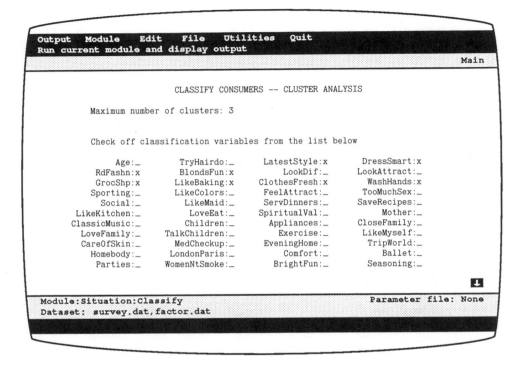

When applied to the information in the survey dataset, it provides a more complete picture of the personalities, interests, and lifestyles of customers in each market segment.

Selecting the Classify Option

The cluster analysis module is loaded by selecting "Module" from the main menu, and then selecting "Situation" and "Classify." The system displays the cluster analysis input template, which lists the maximum number of clusters and the variable names in the survey dataset (Figure 3.11). To select the number of clusters and variables for analysis, the user should select "Edit" from the main menu. The cursor will move to the template area (edit mode).

Selecting the Maximum Number of Clusters

ADSTRAT uses a divisive or "fission" classification procedure. The sample of 300 respondents in the survey dataset is progressively subdivided into smaller and smaller groups until an acceptable number of clusters is obtained. The default value for the maximum number of clusters is five. However, this may or may not be the correct number. It is the user's responsibility to determine the appropriate number of clusters. This decision is based on a number of factors. The user may first have some *a priori* notion about the true number of market segments. He or she may then break the sample of customers into varying numbers of clusters and examine the characteristics of each set of clusters. The user selects a particular solution based on the size and interpretability of the differences between clusters.

To assist the user in selecting the number of clusters, ADSTRAT prints a *t* statistic at each stage in the sample decomposition process (see ahead, Figure 3.13). The *t* value indicates, for the last pair of clusters split by the procedure, the difference between the two clusters' mean values relative to their within-group variances. A small *t* value (less than about 1.5) indicates that there is probably no real difference between the two groups in the total population of consumers. A large *t* value indicates large between-group differences.

The statistical significance of these differences can be determined by comparing the calculated values of *t* and the corresponding degrees of freedom (*df*) with values reported in the *t*-tables of statistics textbooks. However, because ADSTRAT assigns observations to groups in order to maximize between-group differences, the significance of these differences is likely to be overstated. Therefore, these values should be used in combination with other criteria to select the number of clusters. The reader should also note that a difference between groups may be statistically significant but not large enough to be of practical importance. Marketers often derive a relatively small number of clusters even though there is significant heterogeneity within clusters.

Selecting Variables

The cluster analysis template lists the continuous variables from the survey dataset, as shown in Figure 3.11. While in edit mode, the user can select a variable by moving the cursor to a check box and pressing the "space bar." The user can select any number of variables within the memory constraints of the personal computer. In Figure 3.11, eight variables are checked off. The division of cases is based simultaneously on all attributes which have been selected. To cluster observations using the selected variables, the user should "Escape" from edit mode, and then select the "Output" option.

The Cluster Analysis Procedure and Output

ADSTRAT's cluster analysis module groups survey respondents into the specified number of mutually exclusive categories based on respondents' similarity on the set of selected classification variables. The analysis is an adaptation of the POLYDIV procedure described in Williams and Lance (1977).[15] The system first calculates the first principal component of the intercorrelation matrix for the selected variables, and generates the corresponding vector of individual factor scores. These scores are then sorted and assigned to two groups so as to maximize the differences between groups. The process is then repeated on each subgroup to further subdivide the dataset. This technique is especially suitable when the data matrix consists of a large number of cases described by a fairly small number of continuous (interval- or ratio-scaled) attributes.

——————————————— Figure 3.12 ———————————————

Example Output of Cluster Analysis (Screen #1)

```
MainMenu        SaveOutput       PrintOutput
Return to main menu and redisplay module parameters
                                                        Output

                CLASSIFY CONSUMERS -- CLUSTER ANALYSIS

     Cluster #      1     2     3
     Observations  155    68    77

     Centroids

     LatestStyle   2.432 5.368 5.468
     DressSmart    2.381 5.412 5.364
     RdFashn       2.445 5.353 5.351
     BlondsFun     3.916 4.015 3.494
     GrocShp       4.200 3.897 4.000
     LikeBaking    4.213 3.868 3.974
     ClothesFresh  4.439 2.059 5.169
     WashHands     4.413 1.956 5.247

                                                          ⬇

Module:Situation:Classify                    Parameter file: None
Dataset: survey.dat,factor.dat
      Press cursor keys and PgUp/PgDn to scroll, ESC to return to main menu
```

When the module finishes execution, it displays, on the first screen of output, the number of respondents or observations grouped into each cluster and the average score of cluster members on each of the classification variables (also called the cluster "centroids"; see Figure 3.12). These centroids are used to interpret the differences between clusters. On the second output screen, ADSTRAT shows the t values and degrees of freedom discussed above, along with a "dendrogram" illustrating the relationships between clusters (Figure 3.13). A "dendrogram" visually represents the steps in splitting apart the group of respondents into clusters. Groups that separate at a higher level in the dendrogram are less similar than those that break apart at a lower point. For example, the plot in Figure 3.13 indicates that groups 2 and 3 are more similar to each other than they are to group 1.

The program automatically creates a new variable (labeled CLUSTER) indicating the cluster membership of each respondent in the dataset. The clusters which are produced by this analysis may or may not correspond to the five consumer segments defined in Chapter 1. The cluster numbers assigned to each group are arbitrary and have no relationship to the segment numbers which appear in the panel dataset. It is up to the user to determine the association between clusters

—————————————— Figure 3.13 ——————————————

Example Output of Cluster Analysis (Screen #2)

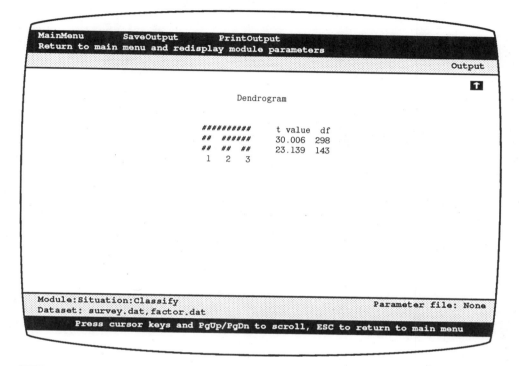

and segments by comparing the cluster attributes from the analysis with the segment descriptions in Chapter 1. The cluster membership variable is automatically saved to disk and becomes available for use in other situation analysis modules. When the user exits the ADSTRAT program, the cluster variable is automatically deleted.

Profile Consumers: Crosstabulation

The next step in analyzing the database of consumer information is to profile the characteristics of consumers. The decision maker needs to develop a complete understanding of the various market segments derived from the cluster analysis in terms of the demographic, psychographic, and decision variables in the survey dataset. The user can also evaluate segments on the general personality and lifestyle dimensions estimated through factor analysis. ADSTRAT provides two tools for profiling consumer characteristics, crosstabulation and regression analysis, which will be discussed in turn.

ADSTRAT's crosstabulation module produces one- and two-way frequency tables. One-way tables are useful for investigating the basic distributional characteristics of each variable. They provide information on an item's variability and central tendency. The decision maker can use frequency tables to assess the general characteristics of the survey sample. For example, one might calculate the total number of people in each age and income group, the percentage of Sonite owners, and the levels of product knowledge of potential customers. One-way tables can also be used to identify questionnaire items with little variation, which might be excluded from other analyses (such as cluster, factor, and regression analyses).

After examining the distribution of each variable, the user can create two-way contingency tables to investigate relationships among pairs of variables. The crosstabulation module displays the joint frequency distribution of cases according to the selected classification variables, which can be either categorical or continuous. This option permits the user to study the differences between clusters in demographics, personality, lifestyles, purchase behavior, decision processes, and media habits.

Selecting the Tabulate Option

The crosstabulation module is accessed by selecting "Module" from the main menu, and then selecting "Situation" and "Tabulate." The system displays the crosstabulation input template, which lists the maximum number of categories, the set of variables in the survey dataset, and the factor and cluster variables (if any). To identify variables for analysis, the user should select "Edit" from the main menu. The cursor will move to the template area (edit mode).

Selecting the Maximum Number of Categories

The user first has the option of specifying the maximum number of categories used to classify continuous variables (such as age, household size, and the various likert-scale questions). When dealing with a continuous variable, the possible values may be too numerous to display individually. Therefore, the crosstabulation module will collapse these values into a set of categories specified by the user. This maximum number of categories is ignored if the value is greater than the actual number of categories, or if the selected variable is categorical (discrete). By default, the maximum number of categories for continuous variables is set to two.

Selecting Variables

The crosstabulation template lists all of the variables from the survey dataset (Figure 3.14). While in edit mode, the user can select a variable by moving the cursor to a check box and pressing the "space bar." The user can select either one or two variables for analysis. In the example shown in Figure 3.14, the variables Marital ("Marital status") and OwnSonite ("Do you currently own a Sonite?") have been checked off.[16] To crosstabulate the selected variables, the user should press "Escape," and then select the "Output" option.

The Crosstabulation Output

If a single variable has been selected, then the procedure displays a one-way

—————————— Figure 3.14 ——————————

Selection of Variables for Crosstabulation

```
 Output   Module    Edit    File    Utilities   Quit
 Run current module and display output
                                                                    Main

                    PROFILE CONSUMERS -- CROSSTABULATION

        Maximum number of categories for continuous variables: 2

        Check off one or two variables from the list below

          Age:_        Marital:x        Income:_           Educ:_
        HHSize:_          Occup:_      TryHairdo:_     LatestStyle:_
     DressSmart:_         RdFashn:_     BlondsFun:_         LookDif:_
    LookAttract:_         GrocShp:_    LikeBaking:_    ClothesFresh:_
      WashHands:_        Sporting:_    LikeColors:_     FeelAttract:_
     TooMuchSex:_          Social:_     LikeMaid:_      ServDinners:_
    SaveRecipes:_     LikeKitchen:_       LoveEat:_     SpiritualVal:_
         Mother:_     ClassicMusic:_     Children:_       Appliances:_
    CloseFamily:_      LoveFamily:_   TalkChildren:_        Exercise:_
     LikeMyself:_       CareOfSkin:_    MedCheckup:_     EveningHome:_
       TripWorld:_        Homebody:_    LondonParis:_        Comfort:_
          Ballet:_         Parties:_   WomenNtSmoke:_       BrightFun:_

                                                                    ⬇
 Module:Situation:Tabulate
 Dataset: survey.dat,factor.dat,cluster.dat        Parameter file: None
```

table reporting the frequency and percentage of observations for each value or range of values of the chosen variable. If two variables were checked off, then the procedure displays a two-way contingency table showing the frequency distribution of the first variable at levels of the second variable (see Figure 3.15). The system also reports the percentage of variables in each cell, the row and column percentages, and a chi-square test of variable independence. The row percentages sum to 100 across columns, and can be used to study the distribution of the column variable at levels of the row variable. Conversely, the column percentages sum to 100 across rows, and indicate the distribution of the row variable at levels of the column variable.

The question often arises as to whether the differences in sample percentages reflect a true relationship in the total population of consumers, or are just due to sampling error. For example, in Figure 3.15, there appears to be a link between marital status and Sonite ownership. People who are married, widowed, or divorced (categories 1, 2, and 3) seem to be more likely to own Sonites than people who are single (category 5). A statistical test of significance tells us the probability that the observed relationship could have happened by chance when there was no true relationship in the population. If this probability

―――――――――――――――― Figure 3.15 ――――――――――――――――

Example Output of Crosstabulation

```
╔══════════════════════════════════════════════════════════════════════╗
║ MainMenu        SaveOutput        PrintOutput                         ║
║ Return to main menu and redisplay module parameters                  ║
║                                                             Output    ║
║                                                                      ║
║              PROFILE CONSUMERS -- CROSSTABULATION                    ║
║                                                                      ║
║                            Marital                                   ║
║  OwnSon          1        2        3        4        5               ║
║         ──────────────────────────────────────────────────          ║
║         :Freq :    67 :     2 :     0 :     0 :    73 :              ║
║       0 :Perct: 22.33 :  0.67 :  0.00 :  0.00 : 24.33 :              ║
║         :Row %: 47.18 :  1.41 :  0.00 :  0.00 : 51.41 :              ║
║         :Col %: 36.61 : 33.33 :  0.00 :  0.00 : 73.74 :              ║
║         ──────────────────────────────────────────────────          ║
║         :Freq :   116 :     4 :    10 :     2 :    26 :              ║
║       1 :Perct: 38.67 :  1.33 :  3.33 :  0.67 :  8.67 :              ║
║         :Row %: 73.42 :  2.53 :  6.33 :  1.27 : 16.46 :              ║
║         :Col %: 63.39 : 66.67 :100.00 :100.00 : 26.26 :              ║
║         ──────────────────────────────────────────────────          ║
║                                                                      ║
║    Chi Square =     47.381                                           ║
║    Degree of freedom =     4                                         ║
║                                                                      ║
║  Module:Situation:Tabulate                      Parameter file: None ║
║  Dataset: survey.dat,factor.dat,cluster.dat                          ║
║     Press cursor keys and PgUp/PgDn to scroll, ESC to return to main menu ║
╚══════════════════════════════════════════════════════════════════════╝
```

is very small (e.g., less than five percent), then we are likely to conclude that the observed relationship is not due to sampling error, but to a true relationship.

The system reports a chi-square statistic which indicates the degree of relationship between the row and column variables. The chi-square value increases as the observed cell frequencies depart from what would be expected if there is no relationship between variables. The probability of obtaining a certain chi-square value by chance alone can be determined by comparing the calculated value and the associated degrees of freedom with values reported in the chi-square tables of statistics textbooks. In the example in Figure 3.15, the chi-square value of 47.381 with 4 degrees of freedom is significant at $p < 0.001$. We would therefore conclude that there is a relationship between marital status and Sonite ownership.

Profile Consumers: Regression Analysis

The second ADSTRAT option for profiling consumers is multiple regression analysis.[17] Multiple regression is used to examine the relationship between a set of independent variables (discrete or continuous) and a single continuous depen-

---
Figure 3.16

Selection of Variables for Regression Analysis (Screen #1)

```
 Output   Module    Edit    File    Utilities   Quit
 Run current module and display output
                                                           Main

              PROFILE CONSUMERS -- REGRESSION ANALYSIS

      Check off independent variables and one dependent variable
      from the list below.

         Independent    Dependent              Independent    Dependent
           Age:_           :_        Marital:_          :_
        Income:_           :_           Educ:_          :_
        HHSize:_           :_          Occup:_          :_
     TryHairdo:_           :_     LatestStyle:x         :_
    DressSmart:_           :_        RdFashn:_          :_
     BlondsFun:_           :_        LookDif:_          :_
    LookAttract:_          :_        GrocShp:x          :_
     LikeBaking:_          :_     ClothesFresh:_        :_
     WashHands:_           :_       Sporting:x          :_
     LikeColors:_          :_     FeelAttract:_         :_
    TooMuchSex:_           :_         Social:_          :_
      LikeMaid:_           :_     ServDinners:_         :_

                                                            ⬇

 Module:Situation:Regress
 Dataset: survey.dat                          Parameter file: None
```

dent variable. This analysis serves both as a descriptive tool, summarizing the linear relationships between the independent and dependent variables, and an inferential tool, allowing one to test the likelihood that relationships observed in the sample would characterize the population.

Regression provides a linear prediction equation that indicates how scores on the independent variables (X_1 to X_k) could be weighted and summed to obtain the best possible prediction of the dependent variable (Y) for the sample. The model can be represented as:

$$Y = \beta_0 + \beta_1 X_1 + \beta_2 X_2 + \cdots + \beta_n X_k \tag{3.1}$$

The system minimizes the sum of the squared distances between the observed values and those predicted by the fitted model. The better the fit, the smaller will be the deviations from the predicted values.

Selecting the Regress Option

To load the regression analysis module, select "Module" from the main menu, and then select "Situation" and "Regress." The system displays the regression analysis input template, which lists the set of variables in the survey dataset (Fig-

---
Figure 3.17

Selection of Variables for Regression Analysis (Screen #2)

```
 Output    Module    Edit    File    Utilities    Quit
 Run current module and display output
                                                          Main

                                                            ⬆

     SaveRecipes:_        :_      LikeKitchen:_        :_
        LoveEat:x         :_      SpiritualVal:_       :_
         Mother:_         :_      ClassicMusic:_       :_
       Children:_         :_       Appliances:_        :_
     CloseFamily:_        :_       LoveFamily:_        :_
    TalkChildren:_        :_        Exercise:x         :_
      LikeMyself:_        :_        CareOfSkin:_        :_
      MedCheckup:_        :_       EveningHome:_        :_
       TripWorld:_        :_         Homebody:_         :_
     LondonParis:_        :_          Comfort:_         :_
         Ballet:_         :_          Parties:_         :_
   WomenNtSmoke:_         :_        BrightFun:_         :_
       Seasoning:_        :_          ColorTV:_         :_
    SloppyPeople:_        :_            Smoke:_         :_
        Gasoline:_        :_         HeadAche:_         :_
         Whiskey:_        :_          Bourbon:_         :_
        FastFood:_        :x      Restaurants:_        :_
     OutForDinner:_       :_      OutForLunch:_        :_

                                                            ⬇

 Module:Situation:Regress              Parameter file: None
 Dataset: survey.dat
```

---

ures 3.16 and 3.17). To identify variables for analysis, the user should select "Edit" from the main menu. The cursor will move to the template area (edit mode).

Selecting Variables

While in edit mode, the user can select a variable by moving the cursor to a check box and pressing the "space bar." The user can select one dependent variable and any number of independent variables for analysis. The dependent variable must be continuous, but the independent variables may be continuous or categorical. In the latter case, the system automatically generates a set of "dummy variables" representing the effect of each level of the variable relative to the last level. For example, the marital status variable has five categories, and would produce four dummy variables labeled Marital_D01, Marital_D02, Marital_D03, and Marital_D04, corresponding to the categories "married," "widowed," "divorced," and "separated."

In the example shown in Figures 3.16 and 3.17, the user has checked off LatestStyle, GrocShop, Sporting, LoveEat, and Exercise as the independent variables and FastFood as the dependent variable. To run the regression analysis, the user should press "Escape," and then select the "Output" option.

--- **Figure 3.18** ---

Example Output of Regression Analysis (Screen #1)

```
 MainMenu        SaveOutput        PrintOutput
 Return to main menu and redisplay module parameters

                                                              Output

                    PROFILE CONSUMERS -- REGRESSION ANALYSIS

      Dependent variable: FastFood

        Source      df      Sum of Squares   Mean Square    F Value    R Square

        Model       5           75.74          15.15         55.92      0.49
        Error      294          79.64           0.27

        Total      299         155.39




                                                                         ↓
 Module:Situation:Regress
 Dataset: survey.dat                              Parameter file: None
       Press cursor keys and PgUp/PgDn to scroll, ESC to return to main menu
```

The Regression Analysis Output

The regression analysis module generates two pages of output (see Figures 3.18 and 3.19). The first page displays a number of general statistics which summarize the fit of the model to the data. The "total sum of squares" represents the total variability in the dependent variable. This is broken apart into: (1) the "model sum of squares," which measures the reduction in variation due to the independent variables in the regression equation; and (2) the residual or "error sum of squares," which is the amount of variation in the dependent variable left unexplained after subtracting the values predicted by the regression model. The "mean square" values are calculated by dividing the sum of squares by the corresponding degrees of freedom (df). The F value is simply the ratio of the model and error mean squares.

The F value is used to test the overall significance of the regression model; that is, whether any of the regression coefficients are significantly different from zero. The calculated F value and the degrees of freedom (df) for the model and error can be compared with values reported in the F-tables of statistics textbooks. In the example shown in Figure 3.18, the F value of 55.92, with 5 and 294 degrees of freedom, is significant at $p < 0.0001$. One might therefore conclude that the

---
Figure 3.19

Example Output of Regression Analysis (Screen #2)

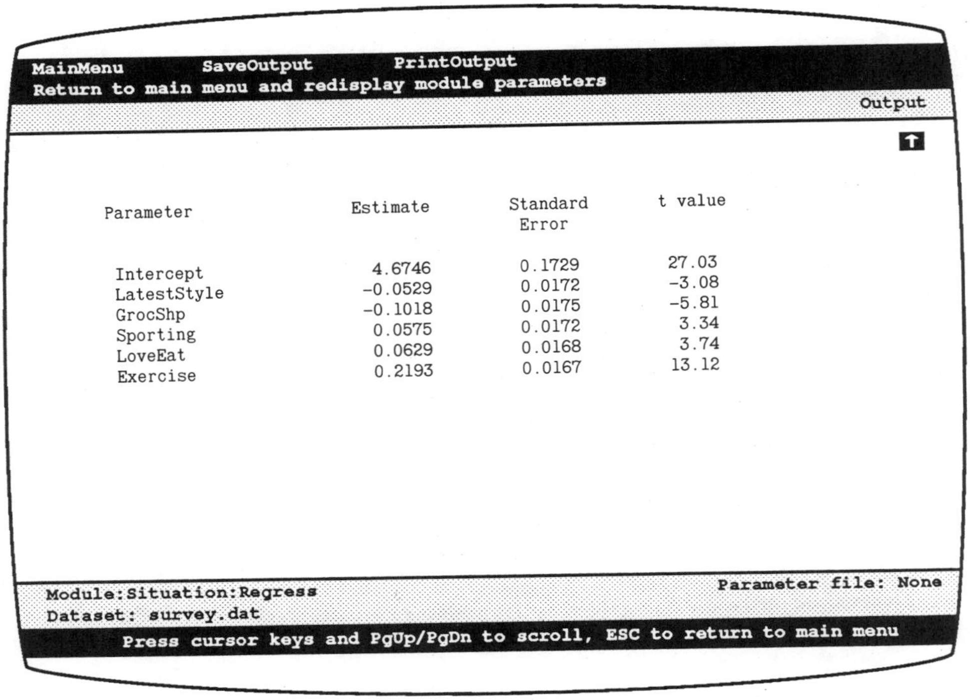

```
MainMenu        SaveOutput       PrintOutput
Return to main menu and redisplay module parameters
                                                              Output
                                                                ⬆

      Parameter          Estimate      Standard      t value
                                         Error

      Intercept           4.6746        0.1729        27.03
      LatestStyle        -0.0529        0.0172        -3.08
      GrocShp            -0.1018        0.0175        -5.81
      Sporting            0.0575        0.0172         3.34
      LoveEat             0.0629        0.0168         3.74
      Exercise            0.2193        0.0167        13.12




    Module:Situation:Regress                    Parameter file: None
    Dataset: survey.dat
         Press cursor keys and PgUp/PgDn to scroll, ESC to return to main menu
```

observed relationship between the dependent and independent variables is not due to chance, but represents a true relationship in the population.

The system also reports an R^2 measure, or "coefficient of determination." This is the proportion of the variance in the dependent variable which is explained by the regression model. R^2 values range from zero to one, where zero indicates no relationship between the predicted and actual values, and one indicates perfect prediction. In general, the higher the value of R^2, the better the model's fit.

On the second page of output, the program displays the estimated parameters of the model and associated test statistics (Figure 3.19). The procedure reports a term for each of the independent variables, and a constant intercept term, representing the predicted value of the dependent variable when all of the continuous independent variables are equal to zero and the categorical variables are set to the last, base level. To test whether each parameter is statistically different from zero, the user can compare the calculated t value and its degrees of freedom with the values obtained from statistics textbooks. For large samples, a coefficient is significant (at $p < 0.05$) if the t value is greater than 1.96. By this criterion, all five of the model parameters shown in Figure 3.19 are statistically significant. From the results of this analysis, it appears that people who frequently eat at fast food restaurants enjoy going to sporting events, eating, and exercise, but do not wear the latest styles and do not like to grocery shop.

When interpreting the results of regression analyses, the user should note that a strong relationship between variables does not necessarily indicate that the independent variables are *causes* of the dependent variable. To establish causality, the researcher must manipulate the independent variables and observe their effect on the dependent variable, ruling out the effects of any extraneous variables.

References

1. In Chapter 5, we discuss how the advertising effectiveness module (econometric analysis) can be used to estimate the strength of the relationships between product and market characteristics and product sales.
2. Note, however, that a cross-sectional analysis provides no information about trends in the data.
3. The industry dataset does not include information at the level of the individual market segment. If the user selects a variable from the industry dataset and requests that the data be subset by segment, this request is ignored.
4. For additional information about factor analysis, the reader should consult Harry H. Harman's 1976 book, entitled *Modern Factor Analysis*, Third Edition, Chicago: The University of Chicago Press.
5. Spearman, C. (1904), "General Intelligence, Objectively Determined and Measured," *American Journal of Psychology*, 15, 201–293.
6. Thurstone, L. L. (1931), "Multiple Factor Analysis," *Psychological Review*, 38, 406–427.
7. Cattell, R. B. (1965), *The Scientific Analysis of Personality*, Harmondsworth, England: Penguin.
8. Kaiser, H. F. (1959), "The Application of Electronic Computers to Factor Analysis," Symposium on the Application of Computers to Psychological Problems, American Psychological Association.
9. Cattell, R. B. (1966), "The Meaning and Strategic Use of Factor Analysis," in *Handbook of Multivariate Experimental Psychology*, ed. R.B. Cattell, Chicago: Rand McNally.
10. ADSTRAT can use up to 640KB of conventional RAM memory. This may limit the number of variables that can be included in the analysis. Check the READ.ME file on the ADSTRAT diskette for additional information.
11. Common factor analysis assumes that only a portion of the variance of each original variable is shared with other variables in the dataset. The estimated factors attempt to account for this common variance.
12. Kaiser, H. F. (1958), "The Varimax Criterion for Analytic Rotation in Factor Analysis," *Psychometrika*, 23, 187–200.
13. If only one factor exceeds the minimum variance criterion, then the system cannot rotate the Initial Factor Pattern matrix.
14. The reader interested in learning more about cluster analysis and its applications should see Punj, Girish and David W. Stewart (1983), "Cluster Analysis in Marketing Research: Review and Suggestions for Application," *Journal of Marketing Research*, 20 (May).
15. Williams, W. T. and G. N. Lance (1977), "Hierarchical Classificatory Methods," in *Statistical Methods for Digital Computers*, eds. Kurt Enslein, Anthony Ralston, and Herbert S. Wilf, New York: John Wiley & Sons, Inc.

16. The second variable appears on the second page of the input template (not shown). It can be displayed by pressing the "Page Down" key.

17. For more information about regression analysis and its application, see Kleinbaum, David G. and Lawrence L. Kupper (1978), *Applied Regression Analysis and Other Multivariable Methods*, North Scituate, MA: Duxbury Press.

4

Communication Objectives

The situation analysis discussed in the last chapter provides a strategic picture of the problems and opportunities facing the brand. On this basis, the marketer must decide on the brand's marketing and communication objectives. The marketing objectives define the brand's target market and describe what is to be accomplished through the marketing program. These goals should be expressed in clear, simple terms and should be stated for a defined time period (such as to stimulate brand trial in the target segment in order to achieve a 12% market share by the end of the year). They should also be consistent with the firm's overall business objectives.

Advertising can play a key role in achieving the marketing objectives. It can stimulate interest in the product category, create brand awareness, build a brand image or personality, differentiate the brand from competitors, and persuade consumers to try the product. A communication objective is defined as "a specific communication task, to be accomplished among a defined audience to a given degree in a given period of time."[1] The communication objectives which are appropriate for a particular brand will depend on consumers' current knowledge, interests, and needs, the brand's attributes, and its position in the market.

Communication objectives provide direction for all of the remaining strategic and tactical advertising decisions. They help the advertiser, the account manager, creatives, media planners, and others involved in developing an ad campaign to work together towards a common goal. This ensures that the right message is communicated to the right group of consumers at the right time and place. Objectives provide criteria for making advertising decisions, and can be used as a benchmark for measuring the quality of results. This feedback allows the advertiser to modify future advertising to increase effectiveness and profitability.

One component of communication objectives is the specification of one or more target audiences. Individuals in the target audience typically include those consumers in the target segment (who are potential purchasers and/or users of

47

the product), as well as people who may influence the purchase decision. A target audience is usually much smaller than the total population of consumers. Even in the case of mass marketed products, such as soft drinks and fast-food, the advertiser often defines a number of target audiences based on differences in regional and ethnic preferences. The target audience should consist of a group of consumers who can be reached with the same advertising medium and will respond to the same message.

To assist the user in selecting communication objectives, ADSTRAT provides three analysis tools. The "ComAssess" option (communication assessment) shows the degree of advertising communication for the brand and its competitors in terms of a hierarchy-of-effects model (see ahead). The "Positioning" option (competitive positioning) displays consumers' brand perceptions and attribute preferences on a multidimensional map. The "Advisor" (objectives advisor) option activates a rule-based expert system, which requests information on brand, customer, and environmental characteristics and then recommends appropriate marketing and communication objectives.

Communication Assessment

Various communication models exist to help advertisers analyze the effectiveness of their messages. Many of these models organize message effects as a series of stages in the communication process, from initial awareness to final action. For example, the AIDA formula suggests that advertising first attracts an individual's attention, then generates brand interest, then desire, and finally a purchase action. The DAGMAR model[2] proposes the stages of awareness, comprehension, conviction, and action, while the Lavidge and Steiner model[3] defines the steps as awareness, knowledge, liking, preference, conviction, and purchase. These approaches are called "hierarchy-of-effects" models because they assume that consumers proceed through these stages in a given sequence.[4]

The hierarchy-of-effects notion provides a useful framework for measuring the extent of communication and defining advertising goals. Clearly, consumers who are unaware of a brand should be exposed to different messages than those who are brand loyal. By surveying consumers on their brand awareness, attitudes, and purchase intentions, the advertiser can determine consumers' existing knowledge and preferences, and decide what needs to be communicated through advertising. For example, if awareness is low, then a reasonable communication objective would be to increase awareness. This might suggest the use of attention-getting advertising. Alternatively, if awareness is high but the brand attitude is negative, then one might attempt to reposition the brand in the minds of consumers so as to increase preference.

ADSTRAT's communication assessment option provides a synopsis of a brand's performance (and the performance of competitive brands) on the various communication dimensions defined by the hierarchy-of-effects model. The three categories of response (cognitive, affective and behavioral) are represented by variables measuring top-of-the-mind brand awareness, brand recognition, brand-attribute knowledge or perceptions, attitudes, purchase intent, and mar-

─────────── **Figure 4.1** ───────────

Case Selection for Communication Assessment Option

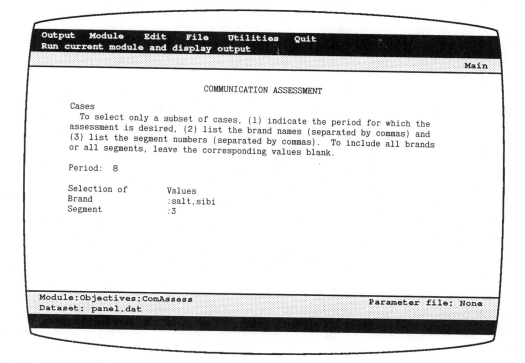

```
 Output    Module    Edit    File    Utilities    Quit
 Run current module and display output
                                                                    Main

                      COMMUNICATION ASSESSMENT
   Cases
      To select only a subset of cases, (1) indicate the period for which the
   assessment is desired, (2) list the brand names (separated by commas) and
   (3) list the segment numbers (separated by commas).  To include all brands
   or all segments, leave the corresponding values blank.

   Period:  8

   Selection of        Values
   Brand               :salt,sibi
   Segment             :3




 Module:Objectives:ComAssess                        Parameter file: None
 Dataset: panel.dat
```

ket share. With this information, the user can diagnose the brand's communication problems and suggest improvements. The data can also serve as a basis for quantifying objectives using the current status of the brand and its competitors as standards of reference.

Selecting the ComAssess Option

The communication assessment module is loaded by selecting "Module" from the main menu, and then selecting "Objectives" and "ComAssess." The system displays the communication assessment input template, which lists criteria for case selection (Figure 4.1). To select the period, brands, and segments for analysis, the user should select "Edit" from the main menu. The cursor will move to the template area (edit mode).

Selecting Cases

The communication assessment option asks the user to select the period, brands, and segments to be included in the analysis (see Figure 4.1). Only one period can be chosen at a time.[5] In this example, the user has selected the most recent (eighth) period. The user can then select the specific brands to include in the analysis by entering the brand names, separated by commas, in the corresponding template field. If no names are entered, then the system will report the data for all of the brands available in the market during the selected time period. In the example shown in Figure 4.1, two brands (SALT and SIBI) have been selected.

Finally, the user may enter the segment numbers for which the assessment is to be performed. If no segment numbers are entered in the template field, then, by default, the system reports information for all of the segments. If, however, the user wishes to display the values of a subset of segments, then he or she must enter the segment numbers, separated by commas, in the associated template field. Figure 4.1 shows an example where data for segment 3 is requested.

The Communication Assessment Output

The output of the communication assessment option shows the performance of competing brands on the various measures of advertising communication according to the hierarchy-of-effects model. Of course, the module can only display information for those variables which are included in the accompanying datasets. ADSTRAT's panel dataset provides information on consumers' brand awareness, perceptions of brands on the three most important attributes (knowledge), purchase intentions, and brand market shares (see Chapter 2). No data were collected on brand recognition and attitudes, so these measures are not displayed in the output.

Example results from the communication assessment option are shown in Figure 4.2. For each of the brands selected (SALT and SIBI), the screen shows the extent of communication on each of the available hierarchy-of-effects measures. If multiple segments are selected, then the system will produce one screen of output for each segment, and the user can browse through them by pressing the "Page Down" and "Page Up" keys.

The results of this example analysis have implications for setting communication objectives. As shown in Figure 4.2, SIBI has a slight advantage over SALT in terms of the proportion of individuals in the segment who are aware of the brand name (79.8% versus 65.7%). However, the relative difference between brands on the purchase intent measure is much larger (12.7% versus 4.2%). Individuals in Segment 3 seem to prefer SIBI, not because of higher top-of-mind brand name awareness, but because they prefer its features, benefits, and/or image. Figure 4.2 reveals that SIBI has higher perceived power (Perc02), but it scores somewhat lower on design (Perc03). One might hypothesize that SALT's market share could be increased by enhancing consumers' perceptions of the brand on these dimensions. To investigate this issue further, the user should study the positions of brands relative to consumers' attribute preferences. This competitive positioning analysis is discussed in the next section.

Competitive Positioning

Marketers are often faced with the problem of understanding why consumers prefer one brand over another and determining how to increase brand preference. One perspective on the brand evaluation process is given by the ideal-

─────── Figure 4.2 ───────

Example Output of Communication Assessment Option

```
MainMenu        SaveOutput        PrintOutput
Return to main menu and redisplay module parameters
                                                              Output

                         COMMUNICATION ASSESSMENT
       Period 8
       Segment 3
       Brand     Awareness Perc01    Perc02    Perc03    Intent   Share

       salt        0.657    5.49      3.25      6.30      0.042    0.030
       sibi        0.798    5.35      3.96      5.82      0.127    0.098

Module:Objectives:ComAssess                          Parameter file: None
Dataset: panul.dat
        Press cursor keys and PgUp/PgDn to scroll, ESC to return to main menu
```

point model. It assumes that buyers have in mind a certain "ideal" brand; that is, they prefer one particular combination of values on a set of perceived product dimensions or attributes. Brands that are positioned close to a customer's ideal will tend to be preferred over brands that are farther away. Marketers can diagnose a brand's condition by plotting the positions of brands relative to consumers' ideal points in a multidimensional attribute space. This is called "perceptual mapping."

To conduct a brand positioning analysis, advertisers will typically identify the brands with which consumers are familiar and the salient attributes or benefits that are important to choice.[6] They will then measure consumers' perceptions of brands on these attributes and their preferences for the attribute levels.[7] The perceptual map is created by plotting the average rating of each brand on each attribute, and the average ideal value of each attribute for each market segment.[8]

ADSTRAT's competitive positioning module generates two-dimensional perceptual maps (see ahead, Figure 4.5). These maps spatially represent the relationships between buyers' perceptions and preferences. They help the advertiser to visualize the position of its brand(s) relative to competitors and relative to the preferences of consumers in each segment. The mapping displayed by ADSTRAT

Figure 4.3

Case Selection for Competitive Positioning Option

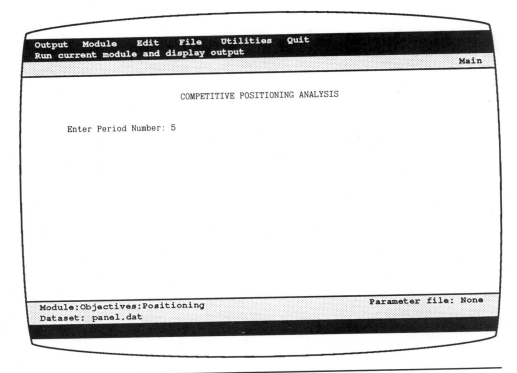

assumes that all respondents perceive the brands in basically the same way, and that the average ideal point for each segment is a generally accurate representation of the preferences of the individual segment members. The maps do not show the differential weighting of the importance of each of the attributes.

The competitive positioning analysis is useful for understanding the structure of the market, for identifying attractive market segments, and for selecting benefits on which to position the brand. Brands that are positioned close together are perceived by consumers to offer the same benefits, and are therefore more competitive. The analysis may reveal under-marketed segments, where segment ideal points exist but no brands currently are located. The advertiser may also target segments that are large or growing, segments that are heavy users of the product, and segments that are especially profitable (e.g., price insensitive consumers).

The advertiser's task is to design ads that either move the brand closer to the ideal points of one or more segments and away from competitors, or to move the ideal points themselves toward the brand. The advertiser will usually *emphasize* those brand benefits that are unique and important, *mention* important benefits that are common across brands, and *leave out* inferior benefits. The advertiser

―――――――――――――――― **Figure 4.4** ――――――――――――――――

Example Output of Competitive Positioning Option (Screen #1)

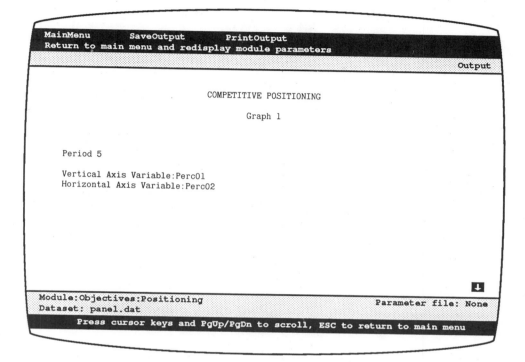

also has the option of introducing an entirely new benefit which is important to consumers, but which is not yet associated with any specific brand (as when ads for 7 Up soft drink first featured the "caffeine-free" attribute).

Selecting the Positioning Option

To access the competitive positioning module, select "Module" from the main menu, and then "Objectives" and "Positioning." The system displays the competitive positioning input template, which consists of only one field, for period selection (Figure 4.3). To indicate the period, select "Edit" from the main menu, and the cursor will move to the template area (edit mode).

Selecting Cases

The competitive positioning option asks the user to select a single time period for analysis (Figure 4.3). Only one period can be chosen at a time. In this example, the user has selected period five. The analysis will include all of the segments and all of the brands on the market at that time.

The Competitive Positioning Output

Figures 4.4, 4.5, and 4.6 illustrate the output obtained from the analysis. The first

─────────────────────── Figure 4.5 ───────────────────────

Example Output of Competitive Positioning Option (Screen #2)

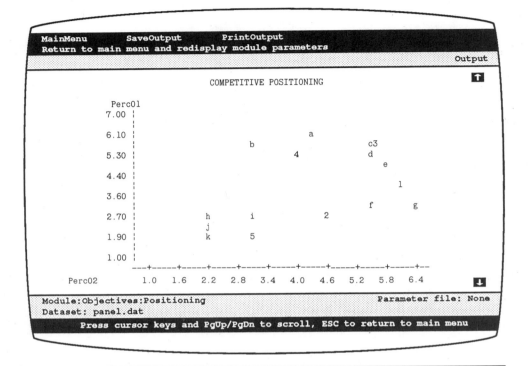

screen shows the selected time period and the labels for the map axes (Figure 4.4). The second screen displays the two-dimensional perceptual map (Figure 4.5). The plotted points represent consumers' perceptions of brands and the preferences of market segments on price (Perc01) and power (Perc02). When three or more attributes or dimensions are included in the database, then ADSTRAT produces one graph for each pairwise combination of attributes. ADSTRAT's panel dataset includes three perceptual variables (Perc01, Perc02, and Perc03), so the system plots Perc01 against Perc02, Perc01 against Perc03, and Perc02 against Perc03. Only the first plot is reproduced in the example. Each map provides a different perspective on the positions of the brands.

The third screen of output shows the legend for the plot (Figure 4.6). Brands are represented by lowercase letters, and the ideal points of each segment appear as numbers. If two or more brands have the same spatial coordinates, then a single letter is plotted. For example, brands SANE and SOLD occupy the same position and are represented by the letter "d."

The map shown in Figure 4.5 indicates that there is greater competition for Segment 3 than for Segment 2, since several brands (SEMI, SANE, SOLD, and SULI) are positioned very close to Segment 3's ideal point and few are nearby

---
Figure 4.6

Example Output of Competitive Positioning Option (Screen #3)

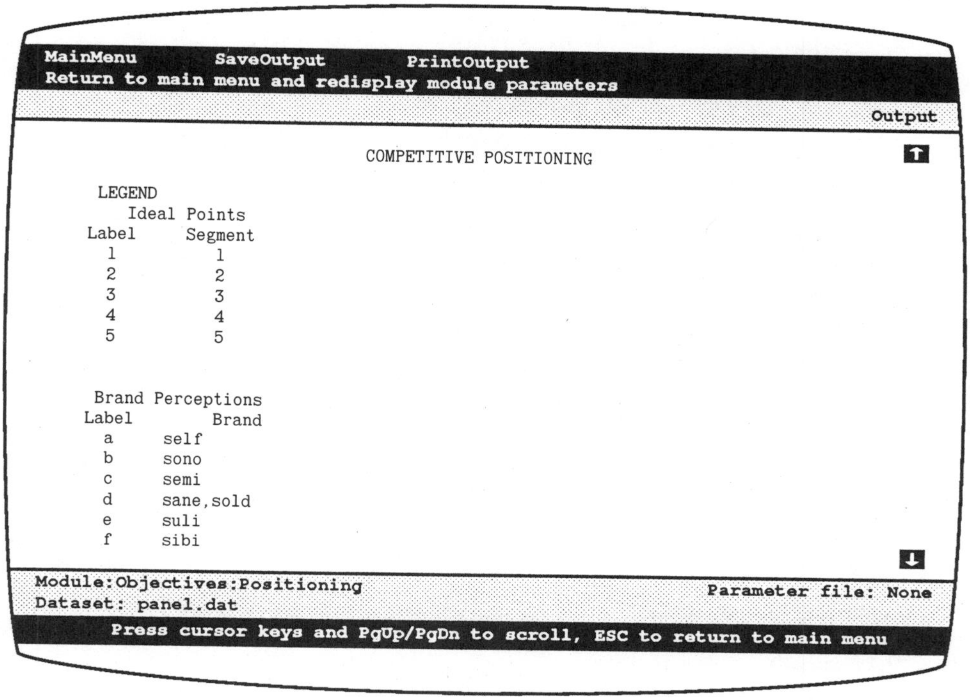

```
 MainMenu        SaveOutput        PrintOutput
 Return to main menu and redisplay module parameters

                                                              Output

                        COMPETITIVE POSITIONING                  ⬆

        LEGEND
          Ideal Points
        Label     Segment
          1          1
          2          2
          3          3
          4          4
          5          5


        Brand Perceptions
        Label        Brand
          a       self
          b       sono
          c       semi
          d       sane,sold
          e       suli
          f       sibi
                                                                 ⬇
 Module:Objectives:Positioning
 Dataset: panel.dat                         Parameter file: None
     Press cursor keys and PgUp/PgDn to scroll, ESC to return to main menu
```

Segment 2. Depending on the size and demand of Segment 2, a firm may find it advantageous to reposition one of its brands closer to this location. For example, the brand represented by point "i" might target Segment 2 by placing more emphasis on its power (Perc02). Of course, the power attribute should be important to this segment and deliverable by the brand.

When interpreting a perceptual map, the user should keep in mind that (1) the map does not display all of the factors affecting consumer choice, (2) small differences in the positions of brands might not be significant given the sample size of the panel, and (3) the perceptual measures may be somewhat unreliable.

An Expert System for Communication Objectives[9]

Quantitative analyses can provide many insights for selecting target markets, positioning brands, and setting communication objectives. However, a considerable amount of knowledge about marketing and advertising strategy is qualitative and heuristic, coming from industry practitioners as well as the academic disciplines of marketing, communications, and the behavioral sciences. This heuristic knowledge can be converted into a set of logical rules and combined with artificial intelligence methodology to create an "expert system." An expert system is an interactive computer program that applies facts, rules, and models in a manner that supports and enhances problem-solving in a specific domain. The term "expert" is intended to imply both narrow specialization and a high level of competence.

ADSTRAT provides two expert system components: the "Advisor" option (objectives advisor) for selecting marketing and communication objectives, and the "Expert" option (advertising design expert system) for identifying promising communication approaches. The objectives advisor module is described in this section, while the advertising design system will be discussed in Chapter 6. Both systems access a knowledge base of problem-solving rules derived from text-books, journal articles, and discussions with advertising practitioners. The system links these rules to the user's description of the situation to draw conclusions. To introduce the user to the system and provide a foundation for interpreting its recommendations, we will briefly review ADSTRAT's heuristics for selecting marketing and communication objectives.

The Knowledge Base

The scope of ADSTRAT's knowledge base covers a wide range of products and services, and is not limited to the Sonite product category or consumer durable goods. The expert system is based on a relatively simple model of consumer behavior. Before purchasing a brand, it is assumed that consumers must: (1) have a salient need to move from their current state to some desired end state, (2) be aware of a brand that can produce this change, (3) be able to identify the brand or discriminate between brands in the product class at the time of the purchase decision, and (4) have no situational barriers to behavior. If one or more of these elements inhibits purchase, then it must be addressed through advertising or other elements of the marketing program. Advertising can stimulate category need, create brand awareness and attitude, facilitate brand recognition and recall, and reduce or remove purchase obstacles.[10]

For new products (especially discontinuous innovations) and for new users of existing products, it is necessary to stimulate primary demand by communicating the benefits that tie the product category to consumers' needs and wants.[11] Likewise, if the product is at the maturity or decline stage of the product life cycle and the brand has a large market share, it may be desirable to increase primary demand, as the brand will reap a large share of the increased category sales.[12] For products that are infrequently purchased (e.g., carpet cleaner) or purchased once and used infrequently, the advertiser should remind the target audience of its need for the product.[13] If consumers are currently users of a frequently purchased product, then one can assume that demand for the product is already present and does not need to be stimulated through advertising.

If the target audience has not used the brand in the past, then the advertiser should attempt to stimulate brand trial. If consumers have used the brand, then advertising should be designed to stimulate repeat purchase or loyalty, or to increase the rate of brand usage. When the rate of product usage is positively related to the quantity purchased (as with snack foods), it may be desirable to directly stimulate purchase. However, when consumers' consumption rate is not influenced by the amount purchased (as with ketchup or gasoline), it is generally less beneficial to have consumers stock up (unless, e.g., the advertiser anticipates heavy competitive activity and is attempting to maintain continuity of purchase). The advertiser should consider alternative objectives, such as increasing brand loyalty by creating or reinforcing positive brand beliefs/image, and/or increasing brand consumption by communicating new brand uses.

Consumer motivation is a key consideration in setting communication objectives. The two basic motivations for product and brand purchase are the need to restore equilibrium from an aversive to a neutral state (negative reinforcement), and the need to increase the level of desirable stimulation (positive reinforcement). The large number of specific purchase motives can be grouped into eight categories.[14] The negative motivations include removing or avoiding a problem, incomplete brand satisfaction, and normal product depletion. Positive motivations include sensory gratification, intellectual stimulation, self esteem, and social approval.[15]

When the motivation is negative, the consumer seeks to overcome or avoid a problem. Advertising can explain how a brand helps to remove the problem and/or offers better performance than the consumer's current brand.[16] This type of advertising has been called "informational,"[17] "thinking,"[18] or "rational/reason why" advertising. When the motivation is positive, the consumer is interested in purchasing the brand primarily to feel good or enhance his/her image. In this case, advertising can communicate a brand image, mood, or the sensory qualities associated with the brand; known as "transformational," "feeling," or "emotional" advertising.

Communication objectives are also a function of the task faced by the consumer at the time of the purchase decision. If the brand decision is made at the point of purchase, then the consumer must be able to recognize the brand (i.e., discriminate between this brand and competing brands).[19] However, if the brand decision is made prior to purchase, then the consumer must be able to recall the brand's name given the product class name or desired benefit as a memory cue (top-of-mind brand awareness). If brand awareness is already high, then it is only necessary to remind consumers of the association between the brand and purchase motivation.

Decision involvement is an important consideration for determining the amount of information to present in ads and the evaluation certainty necessary for choice. Consumer decision involvement is a function of the economic, psychosocial, and physical risk associated with purchasing and/or using the advertised brand. If consumers are currently using the brand, then their decision to repeat the brand purchase is likely to be low involvement.[20] In low involvement situations, consumers may choose a brand based on brand recognition and/or the recall of a few brand benefits.[21] On the other hand, high involvement decisions require lower levels of evaluation uncertainty and decision risk. In the latter case, ads should be designed to communicate sufficient information to support the benefit claims.

Figure 4.7

Problem Definition for Objectives Advisor Option

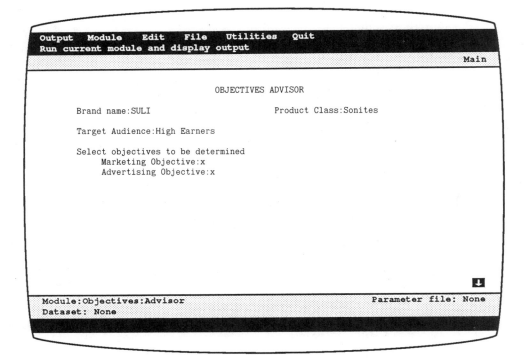

```
Output   Module   Edit   File   Utilities   Quit
Run current module and display output
                                                                Main

                        OBJECTIVES ADVISOR

        Brand name:SULI                    Product Class:Sonites

        Target Audience:High Earners

        Select objectives to be determined
              Marketing Objective:x
              Advertising Objective:x




Module:Objectives:Advisor                    Parameter file: None
Dataset: None
```

Selecting the Advisor Option

The objectives advisor module is accessed by selecting "Module" from the main menu, and then selecting "Objectives" and "Advisor." The system displays the objectives advisor input template, which includes fields for entering the brand's name, product class, and target audience, and for selecting the objective variables for analysis (Figure 4.7). To input this information, the user should select "Edit" from the main menu. The cursor will move to the template area (edit mode).

Defining the Problem

The user must first enter the name of the brand to be advertised, its product class, and the name of the targeted market segment (not the segment number). The user should then select the expert system's goal: to determine the brand's marketing and/or advertising objectives. Either one or both types of objectives can be checked off. In the example shown in Figure 4.7, the user has asked the system to recommend marketing and advertising objectives for brand SULI with respect to the High Earners target audience. To run the expert system, the user should "Escape" from edit mode, and then select the "Output" option. There will

—————————————— Figure 4.8 ——————————————

Consultation with Objectives Advisor

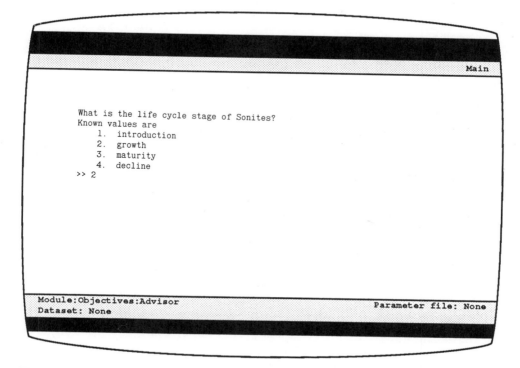

```
                                                                      Main

        What is the life cycle stage of Sonites?
        Known values are
           1.  introduction
           2.  growth
           3.  maturity
           4.  decline
        >> 2
```

Module:Objectives:Advisor   Parameter file: None
Dataset: None

be a short pause, and then the system will begin asking a series of questions about the situation.

The Objectives Advisor Consultation

ADSTRAT attempts to infer the appropriate marketing and advertising objectives by testing the conditions of the various rules in the knowledge base. If the value of a rule's condition is not known and cannot be inferred from other rules, then the system asks the user for this information.[22] For example, to infer that the marketer should attempt to stimulate primary demand for Sonites, the system needs to know whether Sonites are at the introductory stage of the product life cycle. If this information cannot be deduced from the user's past input, the system will display a multiple-choice question asking about the product's life cycle stage (Figure 4.8).

To answer a question, the user should press the number key corresponding to the desired response. For example, in Figure 4.8, the user indicates that Sonites are at the growth stage of the product life cycle by pressing 2 and then hitting the "Enter" ("Return") key. Alternatively, the user can type in the actual response (*growth*) and press "Enter." When the system asks a question in the

─────────────────── **Figure 4.9** ───────────────────

Consultation with Objectives Advisor

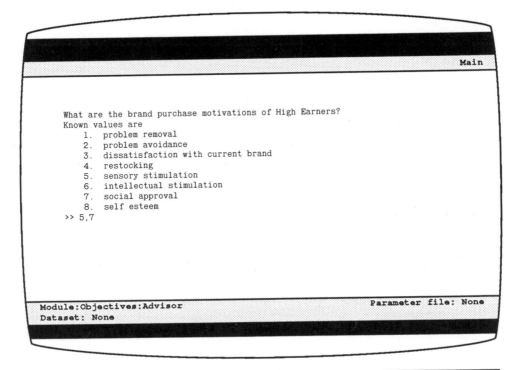

```
                                                                    Main

      What are the brand purchase motivations of High Earners?
      Known values are
            1.   problem removal
            2.   problem avoidance
            3.   dissatisfaction with current brand
            4.   restocking
            5.   sensory stimulation
            6.   intellectual stimulation
            7.   social approval
            8.   self esteem
      >> 5,7




   Module:Objectives:Advisor                      Parameter file: None
   Dataset: None
```

plural form (e.g., "What <u>are</u> the brand purchase motivation<u>s</u> of High Earners?"), the user can enter one or more responses separated by commas (see Figure 4.9). If the system does not recognize the input, it prints "INPUT ERROR: Please re-enter value." Once a response has been correctly entered, the system will proceed to the next question.[23] ADSTRAT only asks for information as it is needed to evaluate the current set of possible objectives. It may ask a different series of questions depending on the user's past answers.

The decision maker's responses to many of the questions should be based on his or her earlier analyses of the industry, panel, and survey datasets. For example, the system may ask for information on consumers' product and brand purchase motivations. These data are reported in the survey dataset and can be displayed using the crosstabulation option (discussed in Chapter 3). Information for other questions may not be available. In such cases, the user must make educated guesses about the correct responses and study their impact on the system's output. Likewise, if ADSTRAT asks a question in a singular form (e.g., "What <u>is</u> the past product usage of High Earners?"), and consumers are actually distributed across a range of values (some people in this segment have used the Sonite

—————————————— Figure 4.10 ——————————————

Example Output of Objectives Advisor

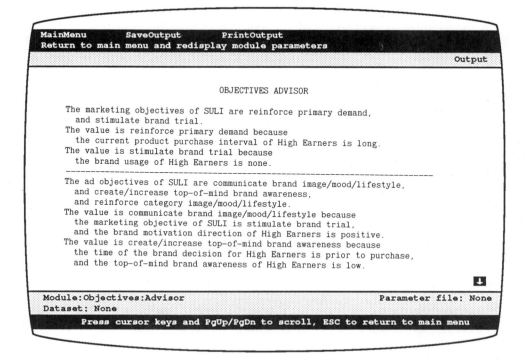

product while others have not), then the user should rerun the consultation with alternative values and observe the effect on the system's recommendations.

The Objectives Advisor Output

At the end of the consultation, the system presents its conclusions for the selected target audience. The system also reports the underlying rationale for each of its recommendations. The decision maker can then conduct a sensitivity analysis by rerunning the consultation, revising the input information, and examining its impact on system recommendations.

In the example shown in Figure 4.10, the system suggests that, because Sonites are infrequently purchased, the target audience (High Earners) should be reminded of its need for the product category. High Earners have never purchased the SULI brand, so the system recommends stimulating brand trial. The audience's motivations for purchasing the brand are sensory stimulation and social approval (Figure 4.9), so ADSTRAT proposes that advertising should communicate a positive brand image, mood, or lifestyle. The system also suggests increasing top-of-mind brand awareness because the brand selection decision is made prior to entering the store, and High Earners are not currently aware of the SULI brand name.

The reader should always keep in mind that ADSTRAT's expert system is designed primarily as a tool for stimulating the user's thinking. The user should critically evaluate ADSTRAT's suggestions and accept, modify, or reject them as appropriate in the particular situation. The recommendations should not be followed blindly.

References

1. Colley, Russell H. (1961), *Defining Advertising Goals for Measured Advertising Results*, New York, NY: Association of National Advertisers, p. 6.
2. Colley, Russell H. (1961), *Opus cited.*
3. Lavidge, Robert J. and Gary A. Steiner (1961), "A Model for Predictive Measurements of Advertising Effectiveness," *Journal of Marketing*, 25 (October), 59–62.
4. There has been some debate about whether these steps are arranged hierarchically. A number of authors have proposed that, when the purchase decision is relatively unimportant, buyers may not have sufficient interest in the product category to develop a strong preference for any particular brand prior to purchase. Instead, a familiar brand is purchased and the brand attitude is formed after consumption. As noted earlier, because of the Sonite's high price and durability, the purchase decision is likely to be highly involving.
5. To evaluate changes in the degree of communication over time, the decision maker can use the trend analysis option of situation analysis, described in Chapter 3.
6. Perceptual maps will be most informative when they are based on the responses of individuals who are familiar with the brands. See Aaker, David A. and Peter Wilton (1984), "Perceptual Heterogeneity: Measurement and Implications," in Proceedings of the 1984 AMA Educators' Conference, Chicago: American Marketing Association.
7. These attributes should be relatively independent of each other to minimize the duplication of presented information and to facilitate interpretation. The attributes reported in the ADSTRAT dataset are not highly correlated.
8. Competitive positioning maps can also be generated directly from consumers' brand preference judgments using multidimensional scaling. A detailed description of scaling techniques is presented in Green, Paul E., Frank J. Carmone, Jr., and Scott M. Smith (1989), *Multidimensional Scaling: Concepts and Applications*, Boston, MA: Allyn and Bacon.
9. Material in this section was adapted from Burke, Raymond R., Arvind Rangaswamy, Jerry Wind, and Jehoshua Eliashberg (1990), "A Knowledge-Based System for Advertising Design," *Marketing Science*, 9 (Summer), 212–229.
10. A related approach is presented in John Rossiter and Larry Percy's (1987) book entitled *Advertising and Promotion Management*, New York: McGraw-Hill. These authors provide a number of heuristics for selecting communication strategies and tactics.
11. Howard, John A. (1977), *Consumer Behavior: Application of Theory*, New York: McGraw-Hill.
12. Benn, Alec (1978), *27 Most Common Mistakes in Advertising*, New York, NY: Amacom.
13. Rossiter, John R. and Larry Percy (1987), *opus cited.*
14. Fennell, Geraldine (1978), "Consumers' Perception of the Product-Use Situation," *Journal of Marketing*, 42 (2), 38–47.

15. The advertiser should distinguish between social approval (a positive motivation), where the brand is purchased to enhance the consumer's image in order to achieve social rewards, and fear of social rejection (a negative motivation), which involves anxiety.

16. Rossiter, John R. and Larry Percy (1987), *opus cited*.

17. Wells, William D. (1981), "How Advertising Works," working paper, Needham, Harper & Steers Advertising, Chicago, IL.

18. Foote Cone & Belding (1978), "How Advertising Works: An FCB Strategy Planning Model," internal report, Foote Cone & Belding.

19. Bettman, James R. (1979), "Memory Factors in Consumer Choice: A Review," *Journal of Marketing*, 43 (Spring), 37–53.

20. Ehrenberg, A. S. C. (1974), "Repetitive Advertising and the Consumer," *Journal of Advertising Research*, 14 (April), 25–34.

21. Krugman, Herbert E. (1965), "The Impact of Television Advertising: Learning Without Involvement," *Public Opinion Quarterly*, 29 (Fall), 349–356.

22. ADSTRAT uses the set of rules in a goal-driven or "backward chaining" fashion, searching from alternative communication objectives back through the rules to conditions to be asked of the user. For more information about expert system methodology, the reader should see Harmon, Paul and David King (1985), *Expert Systems*, New York: Wiley.

23. During the consultation (question and answer) period, the "Escape" key will not interrupt the program's operation. The user must complete the consultation and wait for the system to display its recommendations before attempting to exit ADSTRAT.

5

Advertising Budgeting Decisions

Once the communication objectives have been established, the advertiser must determine a budget for the advertising campaign. This budget should be sufficient to achieve the communication goals, while, at the same time, being consistent with the firm's overall marketing and business objectives (e.g., profit maximization). The decision about how much to spend depends on the emphasis placed on advertising relative to other elements of the marketing mix, the sensitivity of consumers to advertising, and the costs of ad production, media, and research. In the following discussion, we present a framework for evaluating budgeting decisions, and then describe ADSTRAT's tools for selecting a budget.

A Framework for Evaluating Budgeting Decisions

The difficulty in determining the size of the advertising budget lies in the complexity of evaluating the effectiveness of advertising. Clearly, if the audience has little or no response to advertising, then a significant budget for advertising cannot be justified. The decision becomes more complicated when the audience *does* respond to advertising. We cannot simply say that advertising is effective. We need to know how consumers respond at each level of advertising expenditure, and whether this response changes over time.[1] We should also understand the effects of various moderating variables on consumers' response, such as the product's price, distribution, and the level of competition.

Figure 5.1 presents a conceptual framework for evaluating advertising budgeting decisions. As noted above, the audience's response to advertising is the central consideration in setting the budget. It is the process that translates advertising expenditures into brand awareness, brand-attribute perceptions, preferences, sales, and market share. The specific variables of interest to the advertiser are defined by his or her communication objectives.

As shown in Figure 5.1, advertising effectiveness is moderated by five major factors. The first is *advertising dynamics*. Over time, people learn about brands

65

Figure 5.1

A Conceptual Framework for Evaluating Advertising Budget Decisions

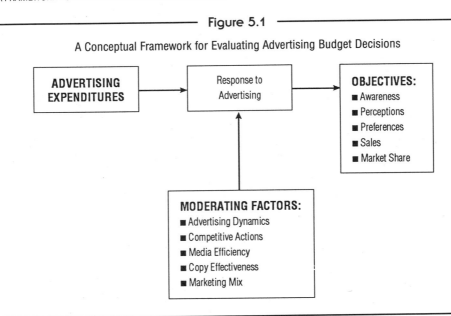

and their characteristics through advertising, the recommendations of friends, and product usage. Consumers' responses to advertising in a given period depend on their prior knowledge of the advertised brand. When advertising stops, sales do not plunge to zero (except, perhaps, in the case of direct-marketed products). There is some inertia in product demand and loyalty patterns. However, without advertising reinforcement, brand information will eventually be forgotten and sales may decrease.

The second factor affecting buyer response to advertising is *competitive actions*. Competitive advertising can attract consumers away from a marketer's brand, reducing the brand's sales and market share. It can also increase the level of media noise or "clutter," thereby reducing advertising efficiency.[2]

A third consideration is *media efficiency*. Different media vehicles are more or less capable of reaching the target audience. Given the high cost of media, significant economies can be achieved through careful media selection. This can make it difficult to compare the advertising budgets of competitors, since one brand may make more effective use of the media than another. Media efficiency is also affected by changes in media costs. As costs increase (due to inflation, increased demand, etc.), efficiency goes down (assuming that audience sizes remain the same).

The fourth moderating factor is *copy effectiveness*. The ad execution can affect the amount of attention paid to the ad and the persuasiveness and memorability of the message. Image-oriented advertising typically requires a higher level of media weight than informational advertising. On the other hand, advertising that features a clearly differentiating feature that is obvious and simple to understand requires less advertising exposure. The copy benefit and usage situations portrayed in the ad can affect the number of people who become interested in the product and their subsequent volume of use. It has been argued that, in some cases, it may be more cost effective to generate a greater variety of creative ad executions than to increase the volume of advertising.[3] Differences in copy effectiveness across brands make it difficult to base an ad budget on competitors' advertising expenditures.[4]

The non-advertising elements of a brand's *marketing mix* can also affect consumer response to advertising. These variables are the fifth budgeting consideration, and include the brand's physical characteristics, price, and distribution. For example, products that are very unique, trendy, and/or provide an important benefit can stimulate a high level of consumer interest, word-of-mouth communication, and sales with only small advertising expenditures. On the other hand, "me too" brands with little differentiation may require a considerable advertising investment to produce a sales increase.[5] The product's price affects both the degree to which consumers respond to advertising,[6] and the profits generated by product sales. The intensity of distribution can have a substantial impact on the potential size of the market, especially for convenience products.

Because of the complexity of the relationship between advertising investments and brand performance, marketers use a variety of methods to determine the advertising budget. ADSTRAT provides three tools for assisting the budgeting decision. The "AdToSales" option reports the advertising expenditures, product sales, and advertising-to-sales ratios of competing brands. The "Effectiveness" option (econometric analysis) estimates the impact of advertising by modeling the relationship between past advertising expenditures and the consequent levels of communication or sales. The user can investigate the strength and shape of the functions linking a variety of predictor variables (including each of the marketing mix variables) with the advertising performance variables (such as brand awareness, sales, and market share). Based on the results of the econometric analyses, the user's past experience, and his/her knowledge of the market, the user can apply the "BudgetAid" (ADBUDG[7]) module to assess the profitability of alternative budgeting plans.

No single analysis tool in ADSTRAT considers all of the factors affecting advertising performance. However, when taken together, these methods provide considerable guidance for the budgeting decision. In the following sections, each of these tools will be described and evaluated in terms of the framework presented in Figure 5.1.

Advertising to Sales Ratios

Two common heuristics for setting an advertising budget are the "percent of sales" method and the "competitive parity" method. A 1981 survey of 55 of the 100 leading consumer goods companies found that over 70 percent of these companies based their budgets on either past or future product sales, and 24 percent attempted to match competitors' spending.[8] Both methods are based on the calculation of advertising to sales (A/S) ratios, defined as the advertising expenditures for a particular brand in a given time period divided by the brand's dollar

---
Figure 5.2

Accessing the Advertising to Sales Ratio Option

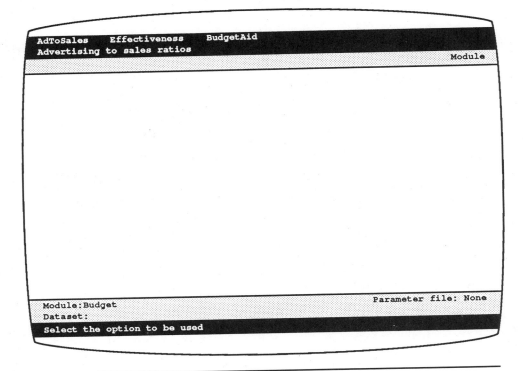

sales during that period. The percent-of-sales method estimates a brand's ad budget by multiplying its past or forecasted sales by its average A/S ratio computed across previous years. The competitive parity method calculates the brand's budget by multiplying its past or forecasted sales by the average A/S ratio computed across competing brands.[9]

The first option for budgeting, AdToSales, presents information necessary for applying the percent of sales and competitive parity heuristics. It displays the advertising expenditures of each brand on the market at each time period, the brand sales levels, and the corresponding advertising to sales ratios.

Selecting the AdToSales Option

The advertising to sales ratio module is accessed by selecting "Module" from the main menu, and then selecting "Budget." Three options are displayed: AdToSales, Effectiveness, and BudgetAid (Figure 5.2). The user should choose the first menu item (AdToSales). The system displays the input template, which lists criteria for case selection. To select cases for analysis, the user should select "Edit" from the main menu, and the cursor will move to the template area (edit mode).

Figure 5.3

Case Selection for AdToSales Option

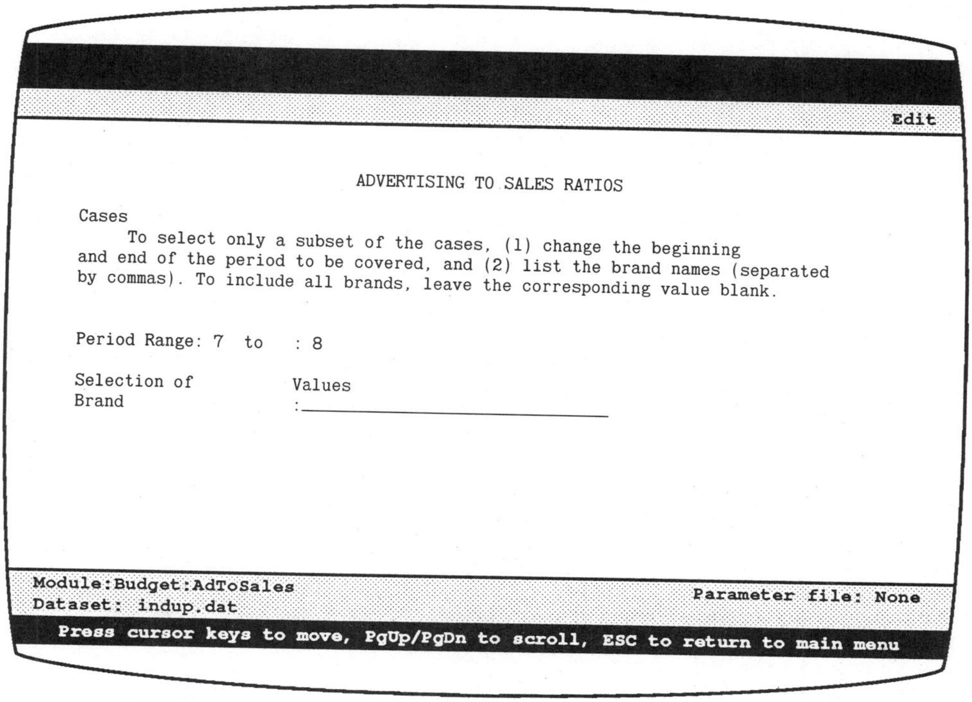

```
                                                                    Edit

                         ADVERTISING TO SALES RATIOS
     Cases
            To select only a subset of the cases, (1) change the beginning
     and end of the period to be covered, and (2) list the brand names (separated
     by commas). To include all brands, leave the corresponding value blank.


     Period Range: 7  to   : 8

     Selection of          Values
     Brand                 :_____




     Module:Budget:AdToSales
     Dataset: indup.dat                          Parameter file: None
     Press cursor keys to move, PgUp/PgDn to scroll, ESC to return to main menu
```

Selecting Brands and Periods

The user can choose the brands and periods for which the advertising to sales ratios will be computed (see Figure 5.3). The user first enters the period range to be analyzed. The default values are the entire range of periods (one through eight) covered by the industry dataset. If a smaller number of periods is desired, the user can enter the starting and ending periods. In Figure 5.3, the user has set the period range from 7 to 8. ADSTRAT also allows the user to select the specific brands to include in the analysis. If the user does not enter a brand name in the corresponding template field (as in Figure 5.3), then the system will perform analyses for all of the brands available in the market during the selected time period. Brands are chosen by typing their respective names, separated by commas, in the corresponding template field. The AdToSales option is run by pressing the "Escape" key to return to the main menu, and then selecting "Output."

The Advertising to Sales Ratio Output

The output of the advertising to sales ratio analysis consists of three parts, as shown in Figures 5.4 to 5.6. The first screen displays the advertising expenditures

---

Figure 5.4

Example Output of AdToSales Option (Screen #1)

```
 MainMenu        SaveOutput        PrintOutput
 Return to main menu and redisplay module parameters
                                                              Output

                          ADVERTISING TO SALES RATIOS

    Brand       Advertising              Period
                7       8     Total
    sama     1000    1200     2200
    salt     3500    3000     6500
    sane     2500    2400     4900
    sark        0    1800     1800
    semi     2000    4000     6000
    sela        0       0        0
    sibi     6000    7000    13000
    siaa    11000    8000    19000
    sold     1000    2000     3000
    sono     2000    3000     5000
    susi     2000       0     2000
    suli        0       0        0
    sulu     3000    4000     7000

                                                                    ⬇

 Module:Budget:AdToSales                         Parameter file: None
 Dataset: indup.dat
        Press cursor keys and PgUp/PgDn to scroll, ESC to return to main menu
```

---

for each brand during the selected periods and the total advertising expenditures by brand across the entire period range (Figure 5.4). The second screen reports the sales (in dollars) for each brand and period, and the total brand sales across the period range (Figure 5.5). The last screen of output (Figure 5.6) presents the advertising to sales ratios (advertising expenditures divided by dollar sales) for each brand and time period, and then averaged across the periods requested. These numbers represent the amount spent on advertising for each dollar of sales. For periods during which a brand is not available, there are no brand sales, and therefore the ratio cannot be computed. ADSTRAT indicates this by printing a dashed line for the corresponding brand and time period (as shown for brand SELA in period 8).

Evaluation of The Advertising to Sales Ratio Approach

The percent of sales and competitive parity methods rely on the assumptions that the market is relatively stable, that firms act efficiently, and that, over time, marketers will arrive at the appropriate levels of advertising spending. Of course, these budget estimates must be adjusted in cases where a brand is just being

─────────────── Figure 5.5 ───────────────

Example Output of AdToSales Option (Screen #2)

```
 MainMenu        SaveOutput       PrintOutput
 Return to main menu and redisplay module parameters
                                                                     Output
                                                                        ⬆

     Brand      Sales                    Period
                 7      8      Total
      sama    28124  34140     62264
      salt    31873  56964     88837
      sane    18140  33691     51830
      sark    22022  33582     55603
      semi   189750 219457    409207
      sela     8045      0      8045
      sibi   352800 447780    800580
      siaa   217211 288000    505211
      sold    76428  83999    160427
      sono    91220 118320    209540
      susi    44962  25696     70659
      suli    49664  39600     89264
      sulu    61865  74340    136205

                                                                        ⬇
 Module:Budget:AdToSales
 Dataset: indup.dat                          Parameter file: None
       Press cursor keys and PgUp/PgDn to scroll, ESC to return to main menu
```

introduced, a brand is making a major repositioning move or reacting to one, or a brand has become established and dominant. As noted earlier, one cannot blindly follow the practices of competitors because they may have different objectives, creative strategies, and media plans, and because consumers may have different amounts of prior knowledge about each of the brands. Moreover, it is hard to know if competitors are, in fact, setting their budgets efficiently.

In terms of the framework shown in Figure 5.7, the advertising to sales ratio approach does consider one aspect of competitive actions (ad spending), and treats sales as the advertising objective (highlighted in italics). Unfortunately, these two variables represent only a small proportion of the factors that should be considered when making the budgeting decision. A fundamental problem with this approach is that it fails to consider that sales are influenced by advertising expenditures, and that sales forecasts should be based on an estimation of consumer response to advertising. As a practical matter, it is difficult to identify the appropriate A/S ratio for a given brand because of the large variance in A/S ratios typically observed across brands within an industry. This approach is more accounting-based than market driven. Nevertheless, it offers a starting point for setting the advertising budget.

Figure 5.6

Example Output of AdToSales Option (Screen #3)

```
 MainMenu       SaveOutput       PrintOutput
 Return to main menu and redisplay module parameters
                                                              Output
                                                                ⬆

     Brand      Ratio                    Period
                 7      8      Avg.
     sama      3.56   3.51    3.54
     salt     10.98   5.27    8.12
     sane     13.78   7.12   10.45
     sark      0.00   5.36    2.68
     semi      1.05   1.82    1.44
     sela      0.00   -----   0.00
     sibi      1.70   1.56    1.63
     siaa      5.06   2.78    3.92
     sold      1.31   2.38    1.84
     sono      2.19   2.54    2.36
     susi      4.45   0.00    2.22
     suli      0.00   0.00    0.00
     sulu      4.85   5.38    5.11


 Module:Budget:AdToSales                  Parameter file: None
 Dataset: indup.dat
       Press cursor keys and PgUp/PgDn to scroll, ESC to return to main menu
```

Measuring Advertising Effectiveness

To determine the appropriate amount to spend on advertising, management must know what level of communication and/or sales will be generated by various levels of advertising in the specific situations faced by the brand. As noted earlier, ad effectiveness should be evaluated in terms of the defined communication objectives. For example, if the objective is to improve brand awareness, then the advertiser should investigate the effects of advertising on awareness. Since the ultimate objective of most advertising campaigns is to increase sales, market share, or profits, these variables are often used as measures of advertising performance.

The relationship between advertising and sales (or communication) can be estimated by experimentation, econometric analysis, or managerial judgment. In an advertising experiment, the volume of advertising is manipulated in different markets or households and the resulting sales levels are recorded.[10] Experiments are the most accurate means of estimating the sales-response function, but they are inherently expensive and time consuming. A less costly alternative is to analyze existing, historical data using econometric methods[11] to identify the

──────────── **Figure 5.7** ────────────

Evaluating the Advertising to Sales Ratio Approach to Advertising Budget Decisions

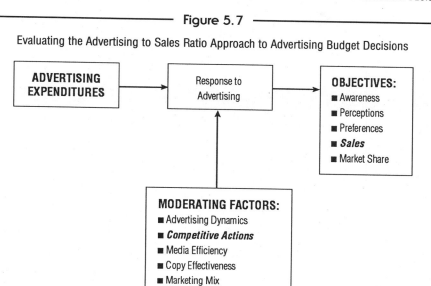

quantitative relationships between advertising, marketing mix variables, competitive actions, environmental factors, and sales. Econometric methods attempt to mathematically isolate the effects of naturally occurring advertising experiments. In cases where there is insufficient variation in the advertising or sales variables, or where a brand was recently introduced and is accompanied by limited performance information, then econometric analysis cannot be applied. Here, the sales-response function can be subjectively estimated by the manager.

ADSTRAT's Effectiveness option permits the user to perform econometric analyses on the industry and panel datasets in order to estimate the relationships between ad expenditures and communication objectives (the left and the right boxes in Figure 5.1). In the following discussion, we present an example to illustrate how the advertiser can model the sales-response function and use this information to guide the advertising budgeting decision.

If one assumes that sales are a constant elasticity response function of advertising with decreasing returns to scale, the sales equation can be written as:

$$S_t = \beta_0 A_t^{\beta_1} \tag{5.1}$$

where:

S_t = Unit sales at period t,

A_t = Advertising expenditures at period t,

β_1 = Advertising effectiveness coefficient (elasticity),

β_0 = Scale parameter.

In this demand equation, the β_1 parameter is the elasticity coefficient; i.e., the

—————————————— Figure 5.8 ——————————————

Case Selection for Effectiveness Option

```
                                                              Edit

                  MEASURING ADVERTISING EFFECTIVENESS

     Cases
            To select only a subset of the cases, (1) change the beginning
     and end of the period to be covered, (2) list the brand names (separated
     by commas) and (3) list the segment numbers (separated by commas).
     To include all brands or all segments, leave the corresponding values
     blank.

     Period Range: 1  to   : 8

     Selection of        Values
     Brand               :_____
     Segment             :_____



                                                              ⬇
    Module:Budget:Effectiveness                Parameter file: None
    Dataset: indup.dat,panel.dat
     Press cursor keys to move, PgUp/PgDn to scroll, ESC to return to main menu
```

percentage change in sales due to a change in advertising expenditures of one percent. The profits generated by these sales are given by:

$$\Pi_t = S_t m_t - A_t \tag{5.2}$$

where, in addition to the definitions above:

Π_t = Profits at period t,

m_t = Gross dollar margin per unit sold at period t.

or, by inserting the sales equation (Equation 5.1) into the profit equation (5.2):

$$\Pi_t = \beta_0 A_t^{\beta_1} m_t - A_t \tag{5.3}$$

We can calculate the advertising level at which profits are maximized by taking the first derivative relative to advertising expenditures and setting it equal to zero:

$$\partial \pi / \partial A = \beta_1 \beta_0 A_t^{\beta_1 - 1} m_t - 1 = 0 \tag{5.4}$$

If one assumes decreasing returns to scale of advertising $(0 < \beta_1 < 1)$, then Equation 5.4 can be solved for advertising, and the optimal budget can be calcu-

─────── **Figure 5.9** ───────

Variable Specification for Effectiveness Option

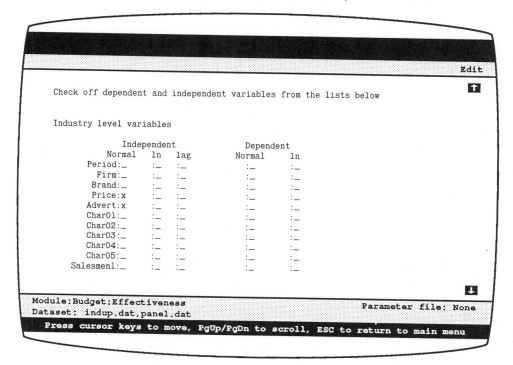

lated. This demonstrates that knowledge of the response coefficient β_1 is critical to the budget decision.

The elasticity notion is also directly applicable to decisions concerning the allocation of resources across the marketing mix. The manager can introduce other marketing variables into the sales response equation, such as salesforce expenditures (personal communication) and the brand's price, along with advertising (mass communication).

For this example, the demand equation is:

$$S_t = \beta_0 A_t^{\beta_1} C_t^{\beta_2} P_t^{\beta_3} \tag{5.5}$$

where, in addition to the variables defined above:

C_t = Personal communication expenditures,

P_t = Brand price,

β_2 = Personal communication expenditures elasticity,

β_3 = Price elasticity.

From the Dorfman-Steiner theorem, it follows that the optimal allocation of a

---
— Figure 5.10 —

Variable Specification for Effectiveness Option (continued)

```
                                                              Edit
                                                               ⬆

        Salesmen2:      :_  :_          :_     :_
        Salesmen3:_     :_  :_          :_     :_
            Cost:_      :_  :_          :_     :_
           Dist01:_     :_  :_          :_     :_
           Dist02:_     :_  :_          :_     :_
           Dist03:_     :_  :_          :_     :_
        UnitSales:_     :_  :_          :x     :_
         DolSales:_     :_  :_          :_     :_
        UnitShare:_     :_  :_          :_     .:_
         DolShare:_     :_  :_          :_     :_
          AdShare:_     :_  :_          :_     :_
         RelPrice:_     :_  :_          :_     :_

    Segment level variables

              Independent            Dependent
         Normal    ln   lag        Normal    ln
         Period:_       :_  :_        :_      :_
                                                               ⬇

    Module:Budget:Effectiveness            Parameter file: None
    Dataset: indup.dat,panel.dat
    Press cursor keys to move, PgUp/PgDn to scroll, ESC to return to main menu
```

---

communication budget to mass communication relative to personal communication is equal to the proportion of the corresponding elasticities;[12] that is:

$$\frac{A}{C} = \frac{\beta_1}{\beta_2} \tag{5.6}$$

ADSTRAT provides econometric techniques for estimating consumer response to advertising in a convenient interactive module. The user can statistically model advertising performance as a function of advertising spending and various other predictor variables. By allowing the user to estimate response elasticities for advertising and other marketing mix variables, ADSTRAT can provide guidance for marketing resource allocation decisions. In the following discussion, we describe the operation of ADSTRAT's Effectiveness module, review model specification issues, and assess the value of this approach in terms of the elements of Figure 5.1.

Selecting the Effectiveness Option

The measuring advertising effectiveness option is loaded by selecting "Module"

─── **Figure 5.11** ───

Variable Specification for Effectiveness Option (continued)

```
                                                                    Edit
                                                                     ⬆
        Segment:       :_   :_           :_      :_
        SegSize:_      :_   :_           :_      :_
        Ideal01:_      :_   :_           :_      :_
        Ideal02:_      :_   :_           :_      :_
        Ideal03:_      :_   :_           :_      :_
         Brand:_       :_   :_           :_      :_
      Awareness:_      :_   :_           :_      :_
        Intent:_       :_   :_           :_      :_
        Shop01:_       :_   :_           :_      :_
        Shop02:_       :_   :_           :_      :_
        Shop03:_       :_   :_           :_      :_
        Perc01:_       :_   :_           :_      :_
        Perc02:_       :_   :_           :_      :_
        Perc03:_       :_   :_           :_      :_
         Dev01:_       :_   :_           :_      :_
         Dev02:_       :_   :_           :_      :_
         Dev03:_       :_   :_           :_      :_
         Share:_       :_   :_           :_      :_
                                                                     ⬇
 Module:Budget:Effectiveness                      Parameter file: None
 Dataset: indup.dat,panel.dat
 Press cursor keys to move, PgUp/PgDn to scroll, ESC to return to main menu
```

from the main menu, and then selecting "Budget" and "Effectiveness." The system displays the first page of the input template (Figure 5.8). The template requests three types of information. The user first selects the cases (or observations) to be included in the analysis. Next, he or she specifies the response function by choosing the explanatory (or independent) variables and the criterion (or dependent) variable from the industry and panel datasets (Figures 5.9 to 5.11). Various data transformations can be performed on these variables. Finally, the user can select between OLS and AR(1) estimation methods (Figure 5.12). To input this information, the user should choose "Edit" from the main menu and the cursor will move to the template area.

Selecting Cases

The first screen of the Effectiveness option allows the user to select a subset of the cases from the industry and panel datasets for analysis (see Figure 5.8). The user first enters the period range. The default values are the entire range of periods (one through eight) covered by the data base. If a shorter time period is desired, the user can enter the starting period and the final period to be covered by the analysis. In Figure 5.8, all eight periods are selected.

Figure 5.12

Estimation Selection for Effectiveness Option

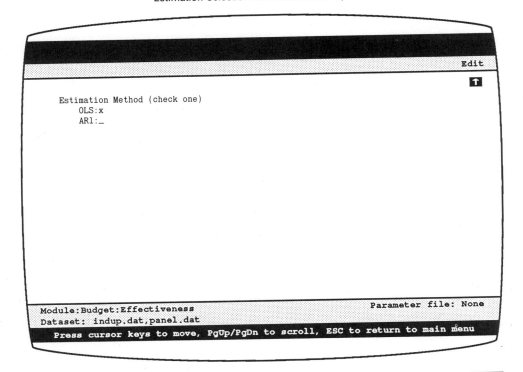

The user can then choose the specific brands to include in the analysis. If the user does not enter a brand name in the corresponding template field, the system will process the data for all of the brands available in the market during the selected time period. This may not be appropriate if the brands compete for different segments or possess different characteristics because their response functions may be different. One way to accommodate this heterogeneity is to run separate analyses on sets of similar brands. At the extreme, the user can enter a single brand name and run a pure time series analysis. However, the number of observations would be limited to the number of periods for which this brand has been available in the market.

If the user is analyzing data obtained from the consumer panel, then he or she can also select the specific segments to be used in the econometric analysis.[13] If no segment numbers are entered in the template field, then, by default, the system processes data for all of the segments. If, however, the user desires to analyze data for selected segments, then he or she must enter the segment numbers, separated by commas, in the corresponding template field.

Selecting the Criterion Variable

Any of the communication and behavior variables described by the hierarchy-of-

─────────────── Figure 5.13 ───────────────

Evaluating the Advertising Effectiveness Method for Advertising Budget Decisions

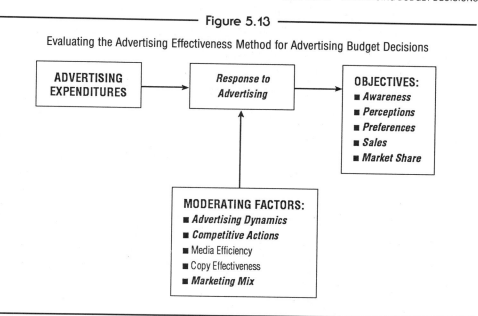

effects model are legitimate communication objectives, and can serve as criterion variables in an econometric analysis (see Figure 5.13). ADSTRAT's industry and panel datasets provide information on:

> Brand Awareness,
>
> Brand perceptions on specific attributes,
>
> Purchase intentions for a given market segment,
>
> Market share, and
>
> Sales.

The user can select the criterion variable by moving the cursor to a check box in one of the two columns labeled "dependent variable" and pressing the "space bar." For example, in Figure 5.10, the variable "UnitSales" was chosen as the dependent or criterion variable, and will be used as the measure of advertising effectiveness. Only a single dependent variable should be checked at a time. This variable must be continuous.

Selecting Predictor Variables

The decision maker should then indicate the set of independent variables that will be used to predict values of the dependent variable (UnitSales). In Figure 5.9, the user has chosen two predictor variables: price and advertising expenditures (Advert). Other elements of the marketing mix could also be included. In fact, the more complete the set of predictors, the better the estimates of the model coefficients. Indeed, if the user accidentally omits variables from the model which are related to the selected independent and dependent variables, then the analysis produces biased estimates of the coefficients. The independent variables may be continuous or categorical. In the latter case, the system automatically generates a set of "dummy variables" representing the effect of each level of the variable relative to the last level.

Specifying the Functional Form of the Relationships

ADSTRAT's Effectiveness module can estimate both linear and certain non-linear relationships between the set of independent variables and the dependent variable. The latter is achieved by performing logarithmic transformations on the original variables. In this section, we review some common models of advertising performance and describe how they would be estimated using the Effectiveness module.

Linear response function. If the user selects untransformed ("Normal") independent and dependent variables, then ADSTRAT performs a multiple linear regression, where the model coefficients indicate the degree of linear relationship between these variables. In the example shown in Figures 5.9 and 5.10, the user has chosen the raw price, advertising, and unit sales variables. Therefore, in this case, the model will be:

$$unitsales = \beta_0 + \beta_1 advert + \beta_2 price \tag{5.7}$$

where:

$unitsales$ = Brand sales in units,

$advert$ = Brand advertising expenditures,

$price$ = Brand price.

The primary advantage of the linear model is its simplicity. The model predicts that each advertising dollar spent creates demand for β_1 units of the advertised brand. However, it is clear that this prediction can only be correct for a small range of the values of the independent variables. The linear model has unrealistic implications at extreme variable levels (e.g., advertising = zero or infinity). An additional concern is that the linear model cannot be used to infer the profit maximizing level of advertising expenditures because the slope of the function is constant. Of course, this is not an issue when the criterion variable is something other than sales or market share.

Constant elasticity response function. The constant elasticity model is extremely common in the marketing and economic literature. The response function is specified as a power function:

$$unitsales = \gamma_0 advert^{\beta_1} price^{\beta_2} \tag{5.8}$$

Taking the logarithms of each side of equation 5.8 and letting $\gamma_0 = \exp\{\beta_0\}$, the following linear relationship appears:

$$Ln(unitsales) = \beta_0 + \beta_1 Ln(advert) + \beta_2 Ln(price) \tag{5.9}$$

This model can be specified and estimated in ADSTRAT by checking the "ln" columns for the independent and dependent variables. These columns are shown in Figures 5.9 to 5.11. When displaying the output, ADSTRAT automatically appends "_Ln" to the names of the transformed variables to indicate that the natural logarithms have been taken.

This model specification has two major benefits. First, the response function shows decreasing (or increasing) returns to scale. This captures the common finding that there are eventually decreasing returns for increased advertising spending. It also overcomes the optimization problems mentioned above for the linear model. The second benefit is that the model does not assume that each independent variable affects the criterion variable independently. Instead, the multiplicative form (Equation 5.8) allows interactions to occur between variables. Therefore, the model can represent the moderating effects of price (and other variables shown in Figure 5.13) on the relationship between advertising expenditures and brand sales. One drawback of this interaction form, however, is that the model predicts that sales are zero with zero advertising.

ADSTRAT also permits the user to transform only the dependent variable, or a subset of the independent variables. While such models would not have constant elasticity responses, their nonlinear forms may be appropriate for some combinations of variables.

Competitive attraction response. As discussed earlier, competitive actions are another factor that affects how the audience reacts to advertising, and should be incorporated in the econometric analysis. In theory, competitors' marketing mix decisions (e.g., advertising expenses, price, salesforce, etc.) could be added as predictor variables to the sales response model. However, these variables are often correlated, which renders the estimated parameters unstable. To sidestep this problem, the user can substitute the brand's relative advertising expenditures (or "share of voice") and relative price (labeled AdShare and RelPrice, respectively, in the industry dataset) for these variables in the model.

An alternative approach is to assume that each brand, through its marketing activities, creates a certain level of goodwill or attraction for the consumer. The consumer's choice of a brand is the result of a comparison of the attractiveness of each brand to all other brands in the market. A brand's market share is therefore equal to the attractiveness of that brand divided by the sum of the attractiveness for all of the competing brands. This formulation provides a logically consistent model of market share,[14] since the predicted shares will always fall between zero and one, and the sum of the market shares for all brands will equal one. The model can be written as equations 5.10 and 5.11:

$$unitshare_{i,t} = \frac{attraction_{i,t}}{\sum_{j=1}^{n} attraction_{j,t}} \tag{5.10}$$

where:

$$attraction_{i,t} = e^{\beta_{0,i}} advert_{i,t}^{\beta_1} price_{i,t}^{\beta_2} \tag{5.11}$$

The competitive attraction model can be estimated with ADSTRAT's Effectiveness option by transforming it to a linear form.[15] To specify this model, the user should select the logarithmic transformation of market share (UnitShare) as the dependent variable and the logarithmic transformations of advertising (Advert) and price as the independent variables. In addition, Brand and Period should be included as independent variables in the model. The Brand variable generates a set of dummy variables (labeled Brand_01, Brand_02, etc.) representing the brand specific intercepts $(\beta_{0,i})$. These intercept terms reflect differences in the intrinsic goodwill of individual brands. The Period variable creates dummy variables (labeled Period_01, Period_02, etc.) reflecting differences in the total market attractiveness (the denominator in Equation 5.10) from one period to the next.

Advertising Dynamics

As indicated earlier, the absence of advertising in one period does not cause a brand's market share, sales, or awareness to suddenly drop to zero. Consumer forgetting and shifts in brand preference occur gradually over time. Likewise, if the manager advertises continuously, the ad exposures have a cumulative effect on the audience. Brand knowledge and purchase interest build up over time.

One way to model advertising dynamics is to incorporate the advertising of the previous period in conjunction with the current advertising expenditures as predictors of the current period sales. This limits the carryover effect to one period, although in some cases this is realistic (for example, when the data are aggregated over long time periods).[16]

A different approach is to assume that, in the absence of advertising, a brand's sales (or market share, awareness, or number of distributors) would drop by a certain percentage after one time period. For example:

$$unitsales_t = \beta_0 + \beta_1 unitsales_{t-1} \tag{5.12}$$

where:

β_0 = Long run minimum sales without advertising,

β_1 = Constant decrease in sales units from period $t - 1$ to t.

We then assume that each advertising dollar spent builds brand sales from this base level. This can be represented by adding an advertising expenditure term to Equation 5.12:

$$unitsales_t = \beta_0 + \beta_1 unitsales_{t-1} + \beta_2 Advert_t \tag{5.13}$$

This model specification can be estimated in ADSTRAT by specifying UnitSales as the dependent variable and selecting two independent variables: (1) advertising (by checking the "Normal" column for variable "Advert") and (2) lagged unit sales (by checking the "lag" column for variable "UnitSales"). When displaying the output, ADSTRAT automatically appends the suffix "_Lg" to the names of the lagged variables. For example, the lagged UnitSales variable would be labeled UnitSales_Lg.

Equation 5.13 can also be taken to represent a "Koyck distributed lag model." This model assumes that sales are a function of all previous periods' advertising expenditures, with an exponential decay in the effectiveness of advertising over time. The reader should note that time series models, like the Koyck model, have a special error structure which affects the selection of the estimation procedure (see below).

Although the example above is linear, other functional forms can be specified. The user can include the logarithmic transformation of a lagged variable by checking both the "ln" and "lag" columns of the appropriate variable. In the output, ADSTRAT uses the convention of appending the suffix "_LL" to the names of transformed, lagged variables (e.g., UnitSales_LL).

Choosing an Estimation Method

The estimation method is specified on the last screen of the input template (Figure 5.12). The default estimation method is Ordinary Least Squares (OLS), which is commonly used for regression analysis. It assumes that, across observations, the error term is independently distributed with constant variance.

However, when times series data are analyzed (as in the case of the Koyck model), it is possible that the errors are correlated from one period to the next, i.e.,

$$e_t = \rho e_{t-1} \tag{5.14}$$

In such instances, the estimation method AR(1) should be chosen, which assumes that the error term is generated by an autoregressive process. It produces unbiased, efficient estimates of the model parameters.

Description of Output

The Effectiveness module generates two pages of output (see Figures 5.14 and 5.15). The displayed information parallels the output of the regression analysis module, discussed in Chapter 3. The first page lists a number of general statistics which summarize the fit of the model to the data. The "total sum of squares" term represents the total variability in the dependent variable, which is decomposed into the "model sum of squares" and the residual or "error sum of squares." The "mean square" values are calculated by dividing the sum of squares by the corresponding degrees of freedom (df). The F value is the ratio of the model and error mean squares.

The F value is used to test the model's overall significance; that is, whether the model's coefficients are jointly significantly different from zero. The calculated F value and the degrees of freedom (df) for the model and error can be compared with values reported in the F-tables of statistics textbooks. In the example shown in Figure 5.14, the F value of 48.17, with 2 and 99 degrees of freedom, is significant at $p < 0.001$. One can therefore conclude that the observed relationship between the dependent and independent variables is not due to chance, but represents a true relationship in the population.

The system also reports an R^2 measure, which indicates the proportion of the variance in the dependent variable which is explained by the regression model. R^2 values range from zero to one, where zero indicates no relationship between the predicted and actual values, and one indicates perfect prediction. In general, the higher the value of R^2, the better the model's fit.

The second screen of the output presents the estimates of the model parameters (the beta's in the equations above) with their standard errors and the corresponding t values. To test whether each parameter is statistically different from

――――――――――――――――――――― Figure 5.14 ―――――――――――

Example Output of Effectiveness Option (Screen #1)

```
  MainMenu          SaveOutput         PrintOutput
  Return to main menu and redisplay module parameters
                                                                   Output


                    MEASURING ADVERTISING EFFECTIVENESS



       OLS Analysis
       Dependent variable: UnitSales

        Source     df    Sum of Squares   Mean Square     F Value    R Square

        Model      2       2.64e+012       1.32e+012       48.166     0.493
        Error      99      2.71e+012       2.74e+010

        Total     101      5.35e+012




                                                                        ⬇

  Module:Budget:Effectiveness                       Parameter file: None
  Dataset: indup.dat,panel.dat
        Press cursor keys and PgUp/PgDn to scroll, ESC to return to main menu
```

zero, the user can compare the calculated *t* value and its degrees of freedom with the values obtained from statistics textbooks. For large samples, a coefficient is significant (at $p < 0.05$) if the *t* value is greater than 1.96. In the example shown in Figure 5.15, the price coefficient, although of the expected sign, is not significant while advertising is shown to have a significant positive effect on unit sales.

In the case of the AR(1) estimation option, the model is estimated in two stages. In the first stage, the same estimation as described above for OLS is used. Therefore the output screens (e.g., Figures 5.16 and 5.17) are the same as for the OLS procedure (Figures 5.14 and 5.15). However, Figure 5.17 offers an additional piece of information associated with time series analysis, the Durbin Watson Statistic, labeled DW. The Durbin Watson statistic indicates the degree of correlation between error terms at periods t and $t - 1$. A DW value of 2 indicates no autocorrelation, a value of 4 represents a perfect positive correlation, and a value of 0 indicates perfect negative correlation. If the value is close to 2, then there is no need to consider the second stage results. If, however the value is substantially greater than or less than 2, then the results of the second stage analysis should be used. The third and fourth screens of output (Figures 5.18 and 5.19)

──────────────── **Figure 5.15** ────────────────

Example Output of Effectiveness Option (Screen #2)

```
┌─────────────────────────────────────────────────────────────────┐
│ MainMenu        SaveOutput        PrintOutput                     │
│ Return to main menu and redisplay module parameters              │
│                                                          Output   │
│                                                            ⬆      │
│                                                                   │
│   Parameter            Estimate       Standard      t value      │
│                                       Error                       │
│                                                                   │
│     Intercept          4.6e+004       6.2e+004       0.742        │
│     Price                  -118            142      -0.826        │
│     Advert                70.2           7.25        9.68         │
│                                                                   │
│                                                                   │
│                                                                   │
│                                                                   │
│                                                                   │
│                                                                   │
│ Module:Budget:Effectiveness            Parameter file: None       │
│ Dataset: indup.dat,panel.dat                                      │
│   Press cursor keys and PgUp/PgDn to scroll, ESC to return to main menu │
└─────────────────────────────────────────────────────────────────┘
```

show the results of the second stage of analysis, which are adjusted using the estimated autocorrelation coefficient, RHO, from the first stage.

Evaluation of the Method

One of the main advantages of this approach is that it summarizes a large amount of data in a set of parameters that have direct implications for advertising and other marketing decisions. This approach can incorporate most of the considerations listed in Figure 5.13. The two remaining factors, media efficiency and copy effectiveness, could also be modeled if standardized measures of these variables were available across brands and time periods.

There are also some difficulties associated with econometric analysis. The parameters which are estimated rely on the specification of the model. If the incorrect model is chosen, then the estimates might be misleading. It is therefore critical for the user to pay special attention to model specification issues. Another problem is that there may be little variation in advertising, which makes it difficult to detect the impact of changes in advertising on sales. The estimates are only valid in the historical range of ad expenditures. If firms have, in the past,

---
Figure 5.16

Example Output of Effectiveness–AR(1) Option (Screen #1)

```
 MainMenu        SaveOutput        PrintOutput
 Return to main menu and redisplay module parameters
                                                              Output


                    MEASURING ADVERTISING EFFECTIVENESS


    AR(1) Analysis
      First Step Results
    Dependent variable: UnitSales

    Source     df    Sum of Squares   Mean Square    F Value    R Square

    Model       2     2.64e+012       1.32e+012       48.166     0.493
    Error      99     2.71e+012       2.74e+010

    Total     101     5.35e+012


                                                              ↓

 Module:Budget:Effectiveness                  Parameter file: None
 Dataset: indup.dat,panel.dat
    Press cursor keys and PgUp/PgDn to scroll, ESC to return to main menu
```

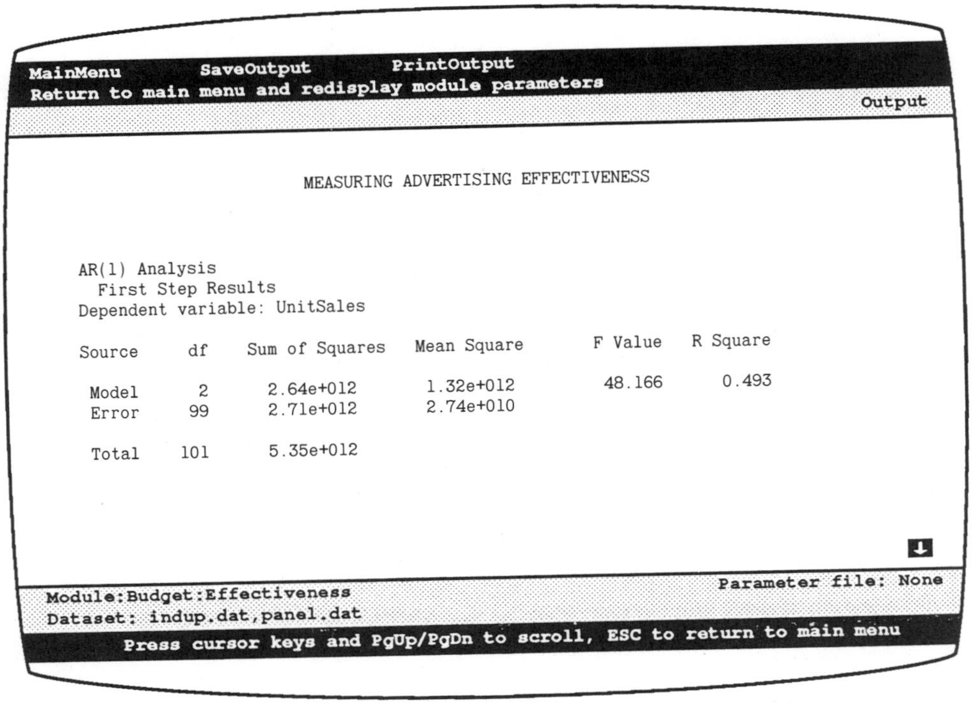

been setting their advertising budgets using a percent-of-sales rule, then the correlation between advertising and sales may be artificially inflated.

Regarding this general econometric approach, Little points out that advertising models should account for certain basic empirical phenomena, which include (among others), the findings that: (1) sales may not be zero with zero advertising, (2) the sales response function is non-linear, and may possibly be S-shaped (i.e., showing regions with both increasing and decreasing returns to scale), and (3) the dollar effectiveness of advertising depends on the copy and media decisions.[17] The budget aid model presented in the next section takes these findings into consideration.

Budget Aid: A Decision Aid Model

While some of the information relevant for advertising budgeting decisions is objective and can be derived from data analysis, other inputs are subjective and uncertain. John Little has argued that a marketing model should incorporate both types of information. He defined the concept of a "decision calculus," which is a model-based set of procedures for processing data and judg-

─────────────── **Figure 5.17** ───────────────

Example Output of Effectiveness–AR(1) Option (Scrreen #2)

```
┌───────────────────────────────────────────────────────────────────────┐
│ MainMenu        SaveOutput        PrintOutput                          │
│ Return to main menu and redisplay module parameters                    │
├───────────────────────────────────────────────────────────────────────┤
│                                                               Output    │
│                                                                    ⬆    │
│                                                                         │
│     Parameter            Estimate        Standard      t value          │
│                                           Error                         │
│                                                                         │
│     Intercept            4.6e+004        6.2e+004        0.742          │
│     Price                   -118             142       -0.826          │
│     Advert                  70.2            7.25         9.68          │
│                                                                         │
│     DW VALUE    1.3355   RHO   0.3322                                   │
│                                                                         │
│                                                                         │
│                                                                         │
│                                                                    ⬇    │
├───────────────────────────────────────────────────────────────────────┤
│ Module:Budget:Effectiveness                      Parameter file: None   │
│ Dataset: indup.dat,panel.dat                                            │
│   Press cursor keys and PgUp/PgDn to scroll, ESC to return to main menu │
└───────────────────────────────────────────────────────────────────────┘
```

ments to assist a manager in his or her decision making.[18] He suggested that, in order for such a model to be useful to managers, it must be sufficiently complete to capture the major response phenomena, but not so complex that the user cannot understand its operation and results. To illustrate this concept, Little developed the ADBUDG model, a decision calculus model for advertising budgeting decisions.

ADSTRAT's budget aid module is an implementation of Little's ADBUDG model.[19] The module gathers information from a knowledgeable user, transforms it into a set of model parameters, and then applies the model to various budgeting scenarios supplied by the user in order to predict sales, market share, and profits.

The budget aid module allows the user to perform a microeconomic analysis of the advertising budgeting decision. This is based on the concept of marginal analysis: that a firm should continue to increase its advertising budget as long as the incremental advertising expenditures are exceeded by the marginal revenues they generate. By searching over the set of possible budgeting alternatives, the user can identify the point at which marginal costs equal marginal revenues, which is predicted to be the optimal expenditure.

─────────────────── Figure 5.18 ───────────────────

Example Output of Effectiveness–AR(1) Option (Scrreen #3)

```
MainMenu          SaveOutput          PrintOutput
Return to main menu and redisplay module parameters
                                                              Output
                                                                ⬆

       Second Step Results
       Source    df    Sum of Squares    Mean Square    F Value    R Square

       Model      2       2.1e+012        1.05e+012      43.152      0.466
       Error     99       2.41e+012       2.43e+010

       Total    101       4.5e+012

                                                                ⬇
 Module:Budget:Effectiveness                       Parameter file: None
 Dataset: indup.dat,panel.dat
       Press cursor keys and PgUp/PgDn to scroll, ESC to return to main menu
```

The Model

The ADBUDG model suggests that a brand's market share at time t consists of three additive components: the brand's long-run market share without advertising, the carryover effects of past advertising, and the incremental effect of current advertising. Consider, first, the effect of a brand's current advertising on its market share. The model makes the following assumptions:

1. If advertising is cut to zero, the brand's market share will decrease, but it will not fall below a certain minimum level by the end of one time period.

2. If advertising is increased to a very high level (saturation), the brand's market share will increase to some maximum value within one time period. This value is probably less than a 100 percent market share.

3. The response function of market share to advertising is either concave or S-shaped.

These assumptions are represented by the following equation:

$$share = min + (max - min) \frac{adv^\gamma}{\delta + adv^\gamma} \tag{5.15}$$

——————————— Figure 5.19 ———————————

Example Output of Effectiveness Option (Screen #4)

```
  MainMenu        SaveOutput        PrintOutput
  Return to main menu and redisplay module parameters

                                                              Output

                                                                 ↑

        Parameter               Estimate      Standard      t value
                                               Error

        Intercept              4.35e+004      5.57e+004      0.782
        Price                      -88.6           118      -0.753
        Advert                      67.2           7.3         9.2



        DW VALUE      1.9883   RHO    0.0058




  Module:Budget:BudgetAid
  Dataset: None                                  Parameter file: None
  Press cursor keys and PgUp/PgDn to scroll, ESC to return to main menu
```

where:

$share$ = Predicted market share after one period with adv advertising,

min = Market share after one period with zero advertising,

max = Market share after one period with saturation advertising,

adv = Advertising rate.

The constants min, max, γ, and δ are derived from market share response information supplied by the user.

This basic model can be expanded to incorporate time dynamics by introducing the notions of long-run minimum share and advertising persistence. The long-run minimum share is defined as the market share that the brand would hold in the long term if the brand was not advertised at all in future periods. Depending on the relative importance of advertising, price, distribution, etc., this value may be greater than zero. Advertising persistence represents the percentage of a brand's market share above the long run minimum that is retained after one period in the absence of advertising. This value is usually less than 100 percent due to competitive activities and consumer forgetting. It is specified as:

$$persist = (min - longmin)/(initialshare - longmin)$$

Figure 5.20

Input for Budget Aid Model

```
                                                              Edit

                        BUDGET AID


     BRAND DATA

        Number of time periods (1 to 12):__
        Market share in period previous to period #1 (% of units):_____
        Market share at the start of period #1 (% of units):_____
        Advertising rate to maintain this market share ($/period):_____
           Estimated market share at the end of period #1 (% of units) . . .
                        with zero advertising:_____
              with the maintenance rate plus 20%:_____
                      with saturation advertising:_____
        Long run market share with zero advertising (% of units):_____
        Average brand price ($/unit):_____
        Contribution profit (before advertising expense) ($/unit):_____


                                                                    ⬇

     Module:Budget:BudgetAid                        Parameter file: None
     Dataset: None
       Press cursor keys to move, PgUp/PgDn to scroll, ESC to return to main menu
```

---

where:

$longmin$ = Long run minimum share,

$initialshare$ = Market share at the beginning of period.

The carryover effect of advertising, then, is simply the fraction of market share above the long-run minimum that persists from one period to the next. Incorporating these dynamics into the response function leads to the model:

$$share_t = \text{longmin} + (persist)(share_{t-1} - longmin) \qquad (5.16)$$
$$+ (max - min) \frac{adv_t^{\gamma}}{\delta + adv_t^{\gamma}}$$

The model can also be extended to include the effects of copy effectiveness and media efficiency discussed earlier in the chapter (see Figure 5.1). The *effective advertising rate* (the term *adv* in Equation 5.16) can be defined as a multiplicative function of advertising expenditures, the quality of the ad copy, and the efficiency of the selected media and vehicles:

$$adv_t = (mediaefficiencyindex_t)(copyeffectivenessindex_t)(advert_t) \qquad (5.17)$$

─── **Figure 5.21** ───

Input for Budget Aid Model (continued)

```
                                                              Edit
                                                               ⬆

  PRODUCT CLASS DATA

    Product class sales at the start of period #1 (units):_____
    Average product price ($/unit):_____

    Consider response to product class advertising?:_
    (If checked, enter the following information)
    Advertising rate to maintain product class sales ($/period):_____
    Product class sales at the end of period #1 (units) . . .
                        with zero advertising:_____
           with the maintenance rate plus 20%:_____
                   with saturation advertising:_____
    Long run product class sales with zero advertising (units):_____



                                                               ⬇
  Module:Budget:BudgetAid                      Parameter file: None
  Dataset: None
  Press cursor keys to move, PgUp/PgDn to scroll, ESC to return to main menu
```

where:

$$adv = \text{advertising rate,}$$
$$mediaefficiencyindex = \text{index of media efficiency,}$$
$$copyeffectivenessindex = \text{index of copy effectiveness.}$$
$$advert = \text{advertising expenditures.}$$

The copy and media effects are represented in the ADBUDG model by indices of copy effectiveness and media efficiency. We assume a reference value of 1.00 for "average" copy and media efficiency. Values greater than 1.00 specify higher than average efficiency, while values less than 1.00 indicate relative inefficiency. For example, a copy index of 1.50 suggests that the copy is 50 percent more effective than normal.

The market share obtained from the model above is then adjusted for non-advertising effects that may vary over time, such as the influence of other marketing mix variables. These effects are represented by a "non-advertising effects" index which has a reference value of 1.00 under normal market conditions. The model can also capture the effects of changes in competitive activity over time by

Figure 5.22

Input for Budget Aid Model (continued)

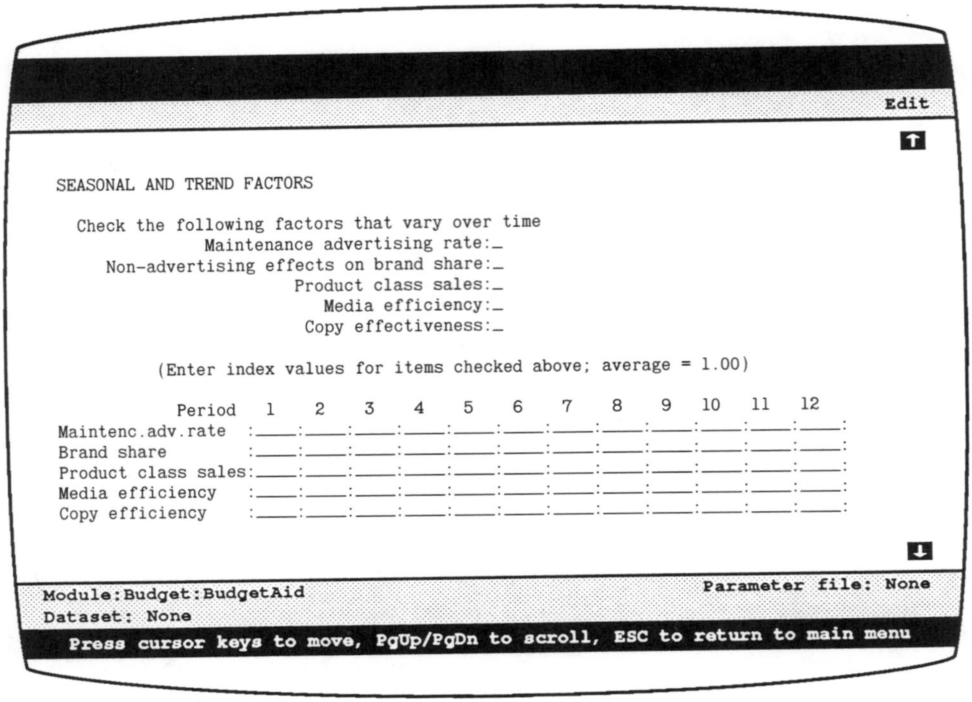

```
                                                                    Edit
                                                                     ⬆

   SEASONAL AND TREND FACTORS

      Check the following factors that vary over time
                   Maintenance advertising rate:_
          Non-advertising effects on brand share:_
                         Product class sales:_
                            Media efficiency:_
                         Copy effectiveness:_

      (Enter index values for items checked above; average = 1.00)

                Period  1    2    3    4    5    6    7    8    9   10   11   12
   Maintenc.adv.rate  :____:____:____:____:____:____:____:____:____:____:____:____:
   Brand share        :____:____:____:____:____:____:____:____:____:____:____:____:
   Product class sales:____:____:____:____:____:____:____:____:____:____:____:____:
   Media efficiency   :____:____:____:____:____:____:____:____:____:____:____:____:
   Copy efficiency    :____:____:____:____:____:____:____:____:____:____:____:____:
                                                                     ⬇

   Module:Budget:BudgetAid                         Parameter file: None
   Dataset: None
     Press cursor keys to move, PgUp/PgDn to scroll, ESC to return to main menu
```

allowing the user to specify a "maintenance advertising rate" index for each period. This index can be set greater or less than 1.00 to indicate that competitive activities are higher or lower in certain periods, and the advertiser must therefore spend more or less to maintain the same market share.

A brand's sales are a function of product category demand as well as the brand's market share. The effects of brand advertising on product class sales can be modeled in the same way as with market share (see Equation 5.16). Of course, the parameters are different for each response function. In addition, sales trends and seasonal changes in product demand are captured by a product class sales index. This index has a reference value of 1.0 for an average sales period, and can vary above or below 1.0 across periods to indicate higher or lower than average sales.

The ADBUDG model can be used to estimate the profitability of a certain level of advertising expenditures. It first calculates the brand's dollar sales by multiplying the brand's price per unit, the predicted brand unit share, and the product class unit sales. It then subtracts out the costs of production and advertising to yield an estimate of the contribution to profits. We now describe how to select and use the budget aid module.

Figure 5.23

Input for Budget Aid Model (continued)

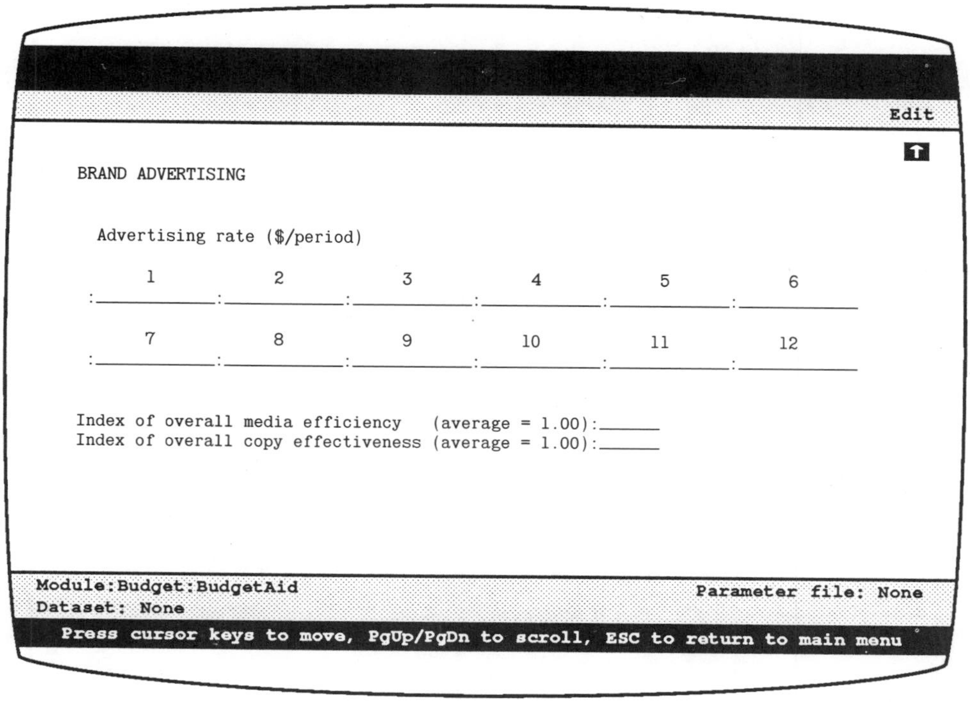

```
                                                              Edit
                                                              ⬆

   BRAND ADVERTISING


     Advertising rate ($/period)

        1         2         3         4         5         6
    :_____:_____:_____:_____:_____:_____

        7         8         9        10        11        12
    :_____:_____:_____:_____:_____:_____


     Index of overall media efficiency   (average = 1.00):_____
     Index of overall copy effectiveness (average = 1.00):_____




   Module:Budget:BudgetAid                    Parameter file: None
   Dataset: None
   Press cursor keys to move, PgUp/PgDn to scroll, ESC to return to main menu
```

Selecting the BudgetAid Option

The budget aid module is accessed by selecting "Module" from the main menu, and then selecting "Budget" and "BudgetAid." The system displays the first page of the input template. To enter information about the brand, product category, and advertising expenditures, the user should select "Edit" from the main menu, and the cursor will move to the template area (edit mode).

Entering Information into the Model

The information necessary for running the BudgetAid option is listed in Figures 5.20 to 5.23. On the first screen of the input template (Figure 5.20), the user provides background information about the brand. The second screen (Figure 5.21) requests similar information about the product class. The third screen (Figure 5.22) concerns factors affecting advertising performance and sales that may change over time. The fourth and final screen (Figure 5.23) asks the user to enter advertising expenditures.

Brand data. The user first indicates the number of time periods to be analyzed. A period unit could represent a year, a quarter, or a month. The budgeting analysis can be conducted over a maximum of twelve periods. In the

---
Figure 5.24

Example of Input for Budget Aid Model

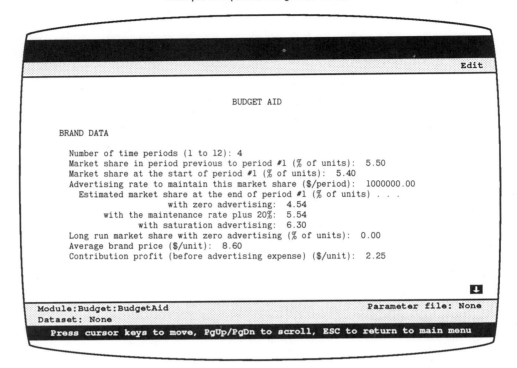

```
                                                              Edit

                           BUDGET AID


      BRAND DATA

          Number of time periods (1 to 12): 4
          Market share in period previous to period #1 (% of units):  5.50
          Market share at the start of period #1 (% of units):  5.40
          Advertising rate to maintain this market share ($/period):  1000000.00
            Estimated market share at the end of period #1 (% of units) . . .
                              with zero advertising:  4.54
                    with the maintenance rate plus 20%:  5.54
                          with saturation advertising:  6.30
          Long run market share with zero advertising (% of units):  0.00
          Average brand price ($/unit):  8.60
          Contribution profit (before advertising expense) ($/unit):  2.25


      Module:Budget:BudgetAid                          Parameter file: None
      Dataset: None
      Press cursor keys to move, PgUp/PgDn to scroll, ESC to return to main menu
```

---

example shown in Figure 5.24, the user has chosen a period range of 4. (Here we assume that the advertiser is developing an ad budget over four quarters.) The user then enters the brand's observed market share in the period previous to the first planning period. All of the user's responses to market share questions should be based on unit sales rather than dollar sales. A 5.5% market share is entered in Figure 5.24.

The next set of questions asks the user to estimate, under various advertising conditions, what the brand's market share would be in a *reference time period*, where the values of all time-varying indices (such as media efficiency and non-advertising effects) are assumed to equal 1.0. The user first enters the brand's market share at the start of the period of analysis. In the Figure 5.24 example, this value (5.4%) is slightly lower than the initial share, indicating that share in the previous period benefited from certain non-advertising effects.[20]

The next four inputs are used to specify the response function (Equation 5.15). The user first gives his or her best estimate of the advertising expenditures (in dollars for one normal period) that would be necessary to maintain the current market share. In this example, the user indicates that it will cost

―――――――――――――――――― Figure 5.25 ――――――――――――――――――

Example of Input for Budget Aid Model (continued)

```
                                                              Edit
                                                                ⬆

    PRODUCT CLASS DATA

      Product class sales at the start of period #1 (units): 22000000.00
      Average product price ($/unit):  8.60

      Consider response to product class advertising?:_
      (If checked, enter the following information)
      Advertising rate to maintain product class sales ($/period):_____
      Product class sales at the end of period #1 (units) . . .
                        with zero advertising:_____
              with the maintenance rate plus 20%:_____
                      with saturation advertising:_____
      Long run product class sales with zero advertising (units):_____



                                                                ⬇
```
Module:Budget:BudgetAid   Parameter file: None
Dataset: None

Press cursor keys to move, PgUp/PgDn to scroll, ESC to return to main menu

---

$1,000,000 in advertising per period to maintain a 5.4 percent market share. The user then estimates: the drop in market share after one period with zero advertising; the increase in market share with a 20 percent increase in advertising spending above the maintenance rate; and the increase in market share with an extremely high level of advertising (saturation). While these judgments might seem difficult to make *a priori,* the user can employ ADSTRAT's other analysis tools to derive better estimates.

The next field (long run market share with zero advertising) asks the user to estimate what the brand's market share would eventually fall to if all future advertising was eliminated. The user should also indicate the average price of the brand, which is used for the calculation of revenues, and the dollar profits per unit, which is used to compute profits.

Product class data. On the next screen, the template asks a number of questions about the product category in which the brand competes. The definition of the product category should be consistent with the market share estimates given previously. The decision maker first specifies the product category sales (in units per period). In the example shown in Figure 5.25, the user has entered 22 million

─────────────────── Figure 5.26 ───────────────────

Example of Input for Budget Aid Model (continued)

```
                                                              Edit
                                                              ⬆

  SEASONAL AND TREND FACTORS

     Check the following factors that vary over time
                    Maintenance advertising rate:x
         Non-advertising effects on brand share:_
                          Product class sales:x
                             Media efficiency:_
                           Copy effectiveness:_

     (Enter index values for items checked above; average = 1.00)

              Period  1    2    3    4    5    6    7    8    9   10   11   12
  Maintenc.adv.rate  :0.80:1.00:1.20:1.00:____:____:____:____:____:____:____:____:
  Brand share        :____:____:____:____:____:____:____:____:____:____:____:____:
  Product class sales:0.85:1.00:1.15:1.00:____:____:____:____:____:____:____:____:
  Media efficiency   :____:____:____:____:____:____:____:____:____:____:____:____:
  Copy efficiency    :____:____:____:____:____:____:____:____:____:____:____:____:

                                                              ⬇

  Module:Budget:BudgetAid                        Parameter file: None
  Dataset: None
  Press cursor keys to move, PgUp/PgDn to scroll, ESC to return to main menu
```

units per period (that is, 88 million units per year). Next, the user enters the average product price per unit. This is the average price across all brands in the product category.

The following questions concern the product class response function; that is, how the total product category sales are influenced by the brand's advertising expenditures. In mature markets where the size of the product category is relatively stable, it is unnecessary to estimate this response. On the other hand, if a brand's advertising has a significant effect on primary demand, then the user should check the item labeled "Consider response to product class advertising?" and enter estimates of product class unit sales per period at each level of advertising. These questions follow the same format as the market share questions discussed above. In the example provided in Figure 5.25, this option is not checked. Therefore, there is no need to fill in responses to the remaining questions.

Seasonal and trend factors. The third template screen is divided into two parts. The first part allows the user to check off those factors that vary over time periods. The second part asks the user to describe the pattern of changes over time. For each factor selected, the user *must* enter information in the correspond-

―――――――――――――――――――――― **Figure 5.27** ――――――――――――――――――――

Example of Input for Budget Aid Model (continued)

```
                                                                 Edit
                                                                  ⬆

    BRAND ADVERTISING


     Advertising rate ($/period)

           1           2           3           4        5          6
    :  800000.00: 1200000.00: 1440000.00: 1200000.00:_____:_____

           7           8           9          10       11         12
    :_____:_____:_____:_____:_____:_____:_____


     Index of overall media efficiency   (average = 1.00):  1.00
     Index of overall copy effectiveness (average = 1.00):  1.00




   Module:Budget:BudgetAid                    Parameter file: None
   Dataset: None
     Press cursor keys to move, PgUp/PgDn to scroll, ESC to return to main menu
```

ing row of the table (for each period in the analysis). If pattern information is entered in the table but the corresponding factor is not checked, then this information is ignored. This facilitates comparison of results with and without seasonal or trend factors.

The budget aid module allows the decision maker to model the effects of the following factors: (1) the maintenance advertising rate (the advertising investment necessary to maintain the brand's market share), (2) non-advertising effects on brand share, such as changes in the other marketing mix variables, (3) product class sales, which may fluctuate due to trends or seasonal variations in demand, (4) media efficiency, which can change over time as a function of media costs and audience size, and (5) copy effectiveness, which may vary due to changes in ad executions or competitive factors, or as a result of advertising wearout.

As noted earlier, the user should use an index of 1.00 to represent the average (reference) value of a variable across the periods. The example shown in Figure 5.26 suggests that the product class sales fall off by 20 percent in the first period, but increase 20 percent in the third period. Likewise, the maintenance advertising rate first drops but then increases, presumably due to changes in competitive activity across time.

--- **Figure 5.28** ---

Example Output of Budget Aid Option (Screen #1)

```
 MainMenu          SaveOutput          PrintOutput
 Return to main menu and redisplay module parameters
                                                                    Output


                                  BUDGET AID


       Period      Share      Brand Sales         Product Sales
                             Units   Dollars      Units    Dollars
                   (%)       (000s)  (000s)       (000s)   (000s)
       ------      -----     ------- -------      -------  --------
         1         5.48       1026    8819         18700    160820
         2         5.61       1234   10615         22000    189200
         3         5.72       1446   12439         25300    217580
         4         5.81       1277   10986         22000    189200

       Total Sales $42860371.17 / 4983764 Units
       Total Product Sales $198000000.00 / 88000000 Units




                                                                        ⬇

 Module:Budget:BudgetAid                           Parameter file: None
 Dataset: None
        Press cursor keys and PgUp/PgDn to scroll, ESC to return to main menu
```

Brand advertising. The budget aid module requests three types of information regarding the brand's advertising. First, the user must enter the advertising expenditures for each time period. ADSTRAT predicts the effects of this spending on market share, sales, and profits. Second, the user specifies the brand's media efficiency index. An average value relative to competitors is 1.00. Finally, the user estimates the effectiveness of the brand's advertising relative to competitors' advertising. A value of 1.00 indicates average advertising.

The Budget Aid Output

The BudgetAid option is run by pressing the "Escape" key to return to the main menu, and then selecting "Output." The module produces two pages of information (see Figures 5.28 and 5.29). The first screen displays the predicted brand market share, sales, and total product class sales (both in units and dollars) for the periods analyzed (Figure 5.28).

The second screen of output (Figure 5.29) presents the predicted contribution to profit per period (before and after removing the costs of advertising), and the cumulative profits across time periods. The last column on the right (labeled "Slope") represents the direction in which advertising spending should be

———————————————————— **Figure 5.29** ————————————————————

Example Output of Budget Aid Option (Screen #2)

```
 MainMenu        SaveOutput        PrintOutput
 Return to main menu and redisplay module parameters
                                                                    Output
                                                                      ⬆

     Period   Contrib   Advertising   Contrib    Cumul     Slope
              before       cost        after     contrib
              advert                   advert
              (000s)      (000s)       (000s)    (000s)
     ------   -------   -----------   -------    -------    ------
              2307.42       800       1507.42    1507.42     0.44
       2      2777.29      1200       1577.29    3084.71    -0.19
       3      3254.48      1440       1814.48    4899.19    -0.49
       4      2874.28      1200       1674.28    6573.47    -0.70

     Total Cost 4640000.00 Dollars




 Module:Budget:BudgetAid                          Parameter file: None
 Dataset: None
     Press cursor keys and PgUp/PgDn to scroll, ESC to return to main menu
```

changed to improve profitability. A slope of zero indicates that the budget for that period is optimal. A positive slope indicates that the advertising expenditures should be increased. A negative slope suggests that the brand is over-advertised, and that spending should be reduced.

For example, according to the information provided in Figure 5.29, the advertising investment of $800,000 in period 1 is too low and the expenditures in periods 2, 3, and 4 are too high. By changing ad spending in the directions suggested by the signs of the slopes and in the amounts corresponding to their magnitudes, the user should be able to increase profits above the current $6.573 million. To illustrate this, a second analysis was run with a new advertising budget. The profit results are displayed in Figure 5.30. The total advertising budget is now much lower ($3.16 million instead of $4.64 million) and yet the cumulative profit has increased to $7.308 million. Note that the slopes are now much closer to a value of zero.

The user should be cautious when using the slope parameters as a guide for setting the budget. They only reflect the estimated profitability of the advertising expenditures over the range of periods specified. Indeed, the example analysis ignores the carryover effects of advertising on sales in periods 5 and after. Con-

―――――――――――――― Figure 5.30 ――――――――――――――

Additional Example Output of Budget Aid Option (Screen #2)

```
MainMenu        SaveOutput        PrintOutput
Return to main menu and redisplay module parameters
                                                              Output
                                                                ⬆

    Period   Contrib   Advertising   Contrib    Cumul    Slope
             before       cost        after     contrib
             advert                   advert
             (000s)      (000s)       (000s)    (000s)
    ------   -------   -------       -------    -------   ------
      1      2408.83     1100        1308.83    1308.83   -0.02
      2      2819.59     1030        1789.59    3098.42   -0.03
      3      2922.04      550        2372.04    5470.46   -0.13
      4      2317.99      480        1837.99    7308.45   -0.47

    Total Cost 3160000.00 Dollars




  Module:Budget:BudgetAid                    Parameter file: None
  Dataset: None
       Press cursor keys and PgUp/PgDn to scroll, ESC to return to main menu
```

sequently, the slope coefficients suggest front loading advertising in the early periods. To avoid this problem, it is recommended that the user define the number of periods to be greater than the advertising planning period. For example, if one is designing an advertising campaign for four quarters, it would be appropriate to specify eight periods to avoid this end-game phenomenon.

Applying the Model

The following steps were suggested by Little[21] on how to use the model:

1. *Set up the model according to the annual plan for the brand.* The objective is to adjust the model so that it reproduces the results found in the original brand plan. This step involves defining the product class sales, including seasonality and product class trends, specifying the advertising-sales response function, and incorporating other factors such as copy and media efficiency.

2. *Update the model on the basis of year-to-date results.* This may require fine-tuning the response function or adjusting the various indices to account for non-advertising effects.

3. *Evaluate new strategies.* Different budgeting plans can then be run to compare their effectiveness in terms of sales, market share, and/or profitability.

4. *Predict future results.* After the evaluation of multiple strategies, one advertising plan should be selected and the model should be run again to estimate the future results.

Evaluating the Budget Aid Approach

The budget aid model gives some consideration to all of the factors indicated in Figure 5.1. In particular, copy effectiveness and media efficiency are represented in the model. Also, unlike the other budgeting approaches discussed earlier, the model clearly displays the implications of various budgeting practices. John Little proposed five additional criteria for evaluating management science models:

1. *Simplicity*—"important phenomena should be put in the model and unimportant ones left out."

2. *Robustness*—"a user should find it difficult to make the model give bad answers."

3. *Ease of control*— "a user should be able to make the model behave the way he wants it to."

4. *Adaptivity*—"the model should be capable of being updated as new information becomes available."

5. *Easy to communicate with*—"the manager should be able to change inputs easily and obtain outputs quickly."

The original ADBUDG model made considerable progress towards satisfying these requirements in the advertising domain. ADSTRAT extends the model on the fifth criterion by providing a highly interactive user interface.

References

1. For a more detailed discussion of these concepts, see Lodish, Leonard M. (1986), *The Advertising & Promotion Challenge: Vaguely Right or Precisely Wrong?*, New York: Oxford University Press, Chapter 6.

2. Burke, Raymond R. and Thomas K. Srull (1988), "Competitive Interference and Consumer Memory for Advertising," *Journal of Consumer Research*, 15 (June), 55–68.

3. Gross, Irwin (1972), "The Creative Aspects of Advertising," *Sloan Management Review*, Fall, 83–109.

4. The same problem exists when attempting to set a brand's ad budget based on its past ad expenditures. If the brand's creative strategy and executions have changed over time, then the current and past situations may not be comparable. See Gatignon, Hubert (1984), "Toward a Theory for Measuring Advertising Copy Effects," *Marketing Science*, 3 (Fall), 308–326.

5. In these cases, marketers often rely, instead, on price promotion to stimulate sales.

6. See, for example, Eskin, Gerald (1975), "A Case for Test Market Experiments," *Journal of Advertising Research*, 15 (April).

7. Little, John D. C. (1970), "Models and Managers: The Concept of a Decision Calculus," *Management Science*, 16 (April), B466–485.

8. Patti, Charles H. and Vincent Blasko (1981), "Budgeting Practices of Big Advertisers," *Journal of Advertising Research*, 21 (December), 23–29.

9. A related approach is share-of-voice budgeting, where the current or desired market share for the brand is multiplied by the total advertising expenditures for all brands in the product category to yield an estimated budget.

10. Eskin, Gerald (1975), *opus cited*.

11. Econometric methods can be applied to two types of historical data: time series data, which record past advertising expenditures and sales over time; and cross-sectional data, which record advertising expenditures and sales for one time period over different brands and/or geographic areas.

12. This allocation rule is also optimal when marketing mix interactions exist. See Gatignon, Hubert and Dominique Hanssens (1987), "Modeling Marketing Interactions with Applications to Salesforce Effectiveness," *Jounal of Marketing Research*, 24 (August), 247–257.

13. As described in Chapter 3, if the user selects variables from the industry dataset and requests that the data be subset by segment, this request is ignored.

14. Bell, David E., Ralph E. Keeney, and John D. C. Little (1975), "A Market Share Theorem," *Journal of Marketing Research*, 12 (May), 136–141. Naert, Philippe and Alain Bultez (1973), "Logically Consistent Market Share Models," *Journal of Marketing Research*, 10 (August), 334–340.

15. Nakanishi, Masao and Lee G. Cooper (1982), "Simplified Estimation Procedures for MCI Models," *Marketing Science*, 1 (Summer), 314–322.

16. Clarke, Darral G. (1976), "Econometric Measurement of the Duration of Advertising Effect on Sales," *Journal of Marketing Research*, 10 (August), 250–261.

17. Little, John D. C. (1980), "Aggregate Advertising Models: The State of the Art," *Operations Research*, 28, January, 629–667.

18. Little, John D.C. (1970), *opus cited*, 16 (April), B466–485.

19. Another implementation of this model was developed by George Day, Gerald Eskin, David Montgomery, and Charles Weinberg (1975), *Cases in Computer and Model Assisted Marketing: Planning*, Palo Alto, CA: The Scientific Press.

20. Users may have difficulty estimating the difference between these two share figures, and should therefore enter the brand's current market share for both questions. We have retained the two inputs to keep the model consistent with the previous implementations described in the literature.

21. Little, John D. C. (1970), *opus cited*.

6

Advertising Copy Design

Advertising performance depends, first and foremost, on the *relevance* of the appeal to the target audience. Effective advertising presents a brand benefit that is important to the audience; a benefit that can potentially satisfy the audience's purchase motivation. John Caples, a direct response copywriter, reports,

> I have seen one advertisement actually sell not twice as much, not three times as much, but 19½ times as much as another. Both advertisements occupied the same space. Both were run in the same publication. Both had photographic illustrations. Both had carefully written copy. The difference was that one used the right appeal and the other used the wrong appeal.[1]

The value of selecting the right benefit is supported by an extensive body of research on consumer attitudes and product positioning.[2] Consequently, marketers carefully study consumers' needs, brand perceptions, and product features in order to select important and unique benefits to be featured in their advertising (see Chapter 4). One must also be sensitive to new trends in tastes, lifestyles, and the environment that might suggest new dimensions for brand positioning.

The second determinant of advertising effectiveness is the *ad execution*. Advertising must communicate the brand benefit in a compelling and engaging way. The advertiser must select stimuli that evoke the desired responses in the target audience, building on the consumer's prior knowledge and experience. There has been a considerable amount of empirical and theoretical research on communication techniques. A number of studies have investigated various mechanical and content factors, including the size and layout of the ad, presenter characteristics, ad format, and the nature of claims mentioned.[3] Ad execution decisions are also based on theories of advertising effectiveness, including the hierarchy-of-effects model,[4] the low involvement model,[5] the elaboration-likelihood model,[6] the Rossiter-Percy communication model,[7] and the resource-matching model.[8]

To make this information available to decision makers, a collection of advertising knowledge was translated into a set of IF THEN rules and incorporated into an expert system for advertising design. ADSTRAT's expert system module applies the knowledge base of published research, communication theory, and practitioner expertise to specific situations, and suggests appropriate communication approaches. It is an extension of the objectives advisor option described in Chapter 4.

The expert system module provides a number of benefits. By asking a series of questions about the brand, competition, consumers, and the environment, the program stimulates the user's creative process by identifying information that is potentially relevant to the decision. It then draws a set of conclusions that can reinforce the user's thinking and/or stimulate the consideration of new alternatives. Through its hierarchical decision process, the system insures that there is a link between marketing and communication objectives and the ad executions.

An Expert System for Copy Decisions[9]

There is considerable skepticism in the advertising community about the value of rules for advertising design. Richard Williams reports, "On one occasion, a new client . . . asked the agency president why all rules for Great Advertising couldn't be codified and stored in a computer bank. Rules that covered every conceivable element of an ad. From concept to execution . . . [the president] couldn't explain why the theory wouldn't have practical application, but it just, well, ah, it wouldn't. He asked the client to trust him."[10] The most common objection to advertising rules, and to research more generally, is that their use may reduce creativity and lead to homogeneous advertising.[11] Advertisers are also concerned that research may not measure some important aspects of consumer response to advertising.[12]

A staunch defender of the use of research in advertising is David Ogilvy. He notes that rules do not provide the magic formula for advertising success, but they can guide advertisers to promising alternatives and help them to avoid egregious mistakes. He argues that many successful advertising campaigns come from inspired use of tried-and-true techniques. "We have observed that the best copywriters and art directors study the research, refer to it, and employ it judiciously as one of the most useful tools of their craft."[13]

The purpose of ADSTRAT's expert system module is to bring advertising theory and research to bear on specific copy decisions. While this research cannot give a complete picture of how consumers will respond to ads, it can provide helpful insights. ADSTRAT selects various advertising communication approaches to achieve the marketing and advertising objectives based on a consideration of consumer, product, and environmental characteristics. These approaches, which include message and presenter characteristics, benefit communication, and the emotional tone of the ad, are briefly described below.[14]

Message characteristics. A large set of rules in the knowledge base selects various message characteristics, including ad format, message arguments, execu-

Figure 6.1

Problem Definition for Expert System Option (Screen #1)

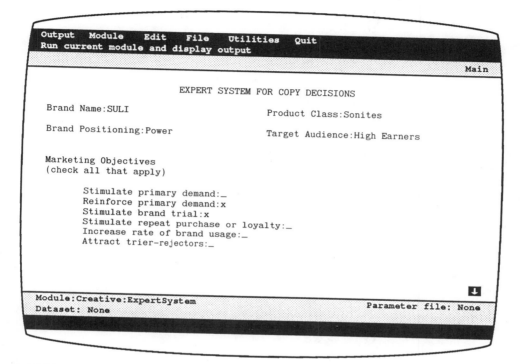

tional techniques, and layout. The system recommends techniques for enhancing brand identification (recognition and top-of-mind awareness), communicating brand information, and increasing brand evaluation. ADSTRAT attempts to match the cognitive resources required for ad processing with the cognitive resources available. This ensures that consumers will understand and react to the key brand message.[15]

Presenter characteristics. The target audience's response to an ad depends on the characteristics of the presenter as well as the message he or she delivers. ADSTRAT determines the expertise, objectivity, attractiveness, and similarity of the presenter by considering the brand's advertising objectives and relative performance, and consumers' purchase motivations, message processing ability, decision involvement, and brand attitude. The system also makes suggestions concerning the age, sex, and identity of the presenter.

Benefit communication. The system determines what emphasis should be placed on the selected benefit by considering the benefit's importance, the degree to which the brand delivers the benefit, and the distinctiveness of the benefit relative to other brands.[16] The system also suggests whether the ad should

---

Figure 6.2

Problem Definition for Expert System Option (Screen #2)

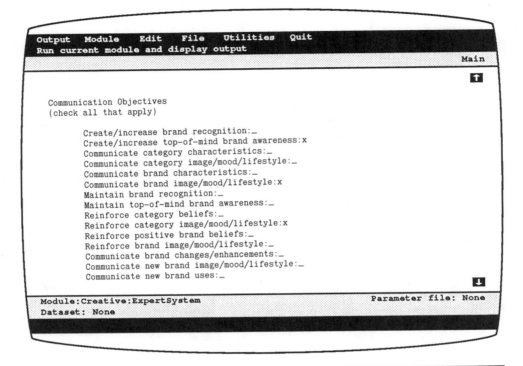

```
  Output    Module    Edit    File    Utilities    Quit
  Run current module and display output
                                                              Main

                                                               ⬆

     Communication Objectives
     (check all that apply)

          Create/increase brand recognition:_
          Create/increase top-of-mind brand awareness:x
          Communicate category characteristics:_
          Communicate category image/mood/lifestyle:_
          Communicate brand characteristics:_
          Communicate brand image/mood/lifestyle:x
          Maintain brand recognition:_
          Maintain top-of-mind brand awareness:_
          Reinforce category beliefs:_
          Reinforce category image/mood/lifestyle:x
          Reinforce positive brand beliefs:_
          Reinforce brand image/mood/lifestyle:_
          Communicate brand changes/enhancements:_
          Communicate new brand image/mood/lifestyle:_
          Communicate new brand uses:_
                                                               ⬇

  Module:Creative:ExpertSystem              Parameter file: None
  Dataset: None
```

---

directly or indirectly compare the brand to one or more competitors, and determines whether a one-sided or two-sided message should be considered.

Message emotion. The last major dimension on which ADSTRAT makes recommendations is the emotional tone of the advertisement. The brand's characteristics, consumer purchase motivations, and ad format dictate the specific tone of the message. When an informational creative strategy is used, ADSTRAT selects a message emotion to support the main selling proposition. If message processing motivation is low, the system advises the advertiser to arouse a strong emotional response (positive or negative) in order to stimulate message processing.[17] When the creative strategy calls for transformational advertising, ADSTRAT recommends conveying the brand's image, mood, or sensory qualities in an appealing way, portraying what the consumer might feel when using the brand.

Selecting the ExpertSystem Option

The expert system for copy decisions is accessed by selecting "Module" from the main menu, and then selecting "Creative" and "ExpertSystem." The system displays the expert system input template, which includes fields for entering the brand's name, product class, positioning, target audience, and objectives, and

Figure 6.3

Problem Definition for Expert System Option (Screen #3)

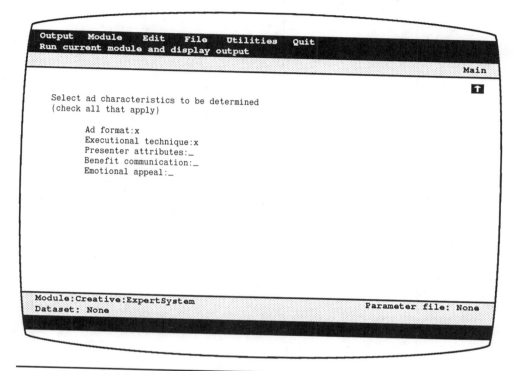

for selecting the advertising design variables to be determined (Figures 6.1, 6.2, and 6.3). To input this information, the user should select "Edit" from the main menu. The cursor will move to the template area (edit mode).

Defining the Problem

As in the objectives advisor module, the user must first enter the name of the brand to be advertised, its product class, and the name of the targeted market segment. In addition, the user indicates the primary benefit on which the brand will be positioned. This decision is based on the situation analysis discussed in Chapter 3, and the competitive positioning analysis of Chapter 4.

The marketing and communication objectives from Chapter 4 provide direction for ad design. This information is entered in the first and second screens of the input template (Figures 6.1 and 6.2, respectively). Any number of objectives may be checked off. However, the total number of communication objectives should be kept small because advertisements can only convey a limited amount of information. Also, the user should avoid selecting conflicting objectives, because this may cause the system to produce inconsistent ad design recommendations. The example shows that the user has selected

Figure 6.4

Consultation with Expert System

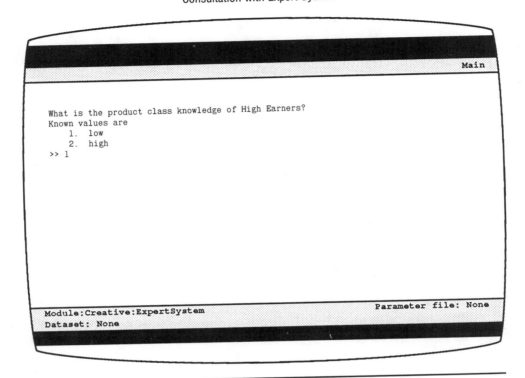

```
                                                                    Main

    What is the product class knowledge of High Earners?
    Known values are
        1.  low
        2.  high
    >> 1




    Module:Creative:ExpertSystem                    Parameter file: None
    Dataset: None
```

objectives based on the earlier output of the objectives advisor module (see Figure 4.10).

The user then selects the expert system's goal. ADSTRAT can recommend ad formats, executional techniques, presenter attributes, emotional appeals, and methods for communicating brand benefits. Any number of message characteristics can be checked off. The greater the number of items selected, the longer will be the subsequent consultation (question-and-answer) period. In the example shown in Figure 6.3, the user has asked the system to recommend ad formats and executional techniques for brand SULI with respect to the High Earners target audience. To run the expert system, the user presses "Escape," and then selects the "Output" option. There will be a short pause, and then the system will begin asking a series of questions.

The Expert System Consultation

ADSTRAT attempts to infer the appropriate communication approaches by testing the conditions of the various rules in the knowledge base. If the value of a rule's condition is not known and cannot be inferred from other rules or the user's past responses, then the system asks the user for this information (Figure 6.4).

───────────────── Figure 6.5 ─────────────────

Example Output of Expert System (Screen #1)

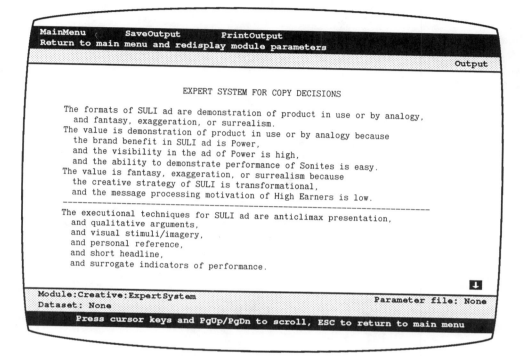

To answer a question, the user should press the number key corresponding to the desired response. For example, in Figure 6.4, the user indicates that High Earners have little knowledge about the Sonite product class by pressing 1 and then hitting the "Enter" ("Return") key. Alternatively, the user can type in the actual response (*low*) and press "Enter." When the system asks a question in the plural form, the user can enter one or more responses separated by commas. If the information is typed incorrectly, the system prints "INPUT ERROR: Please re-enter value." Once a legal response has been entered, the system will proceed to the next question.[18] ADSTRAT only asks for information as it is needed, and may ask a different series of questions depending on the user's past answers. The decision maker's responses to the questions should be based on his or her earlier analyses of the industry, panel, and survey datasets.

The Expert System Output

At the end of the consultation, the system presents its conclusions for the selected target audience and reports the underlying rationale for each of its recommendations. In the example shown in Figures 6.5 and 6.6, the system suggests that the SULI brand be demonstrated in use or by analogy to illustrate

---
Figure 6.6

Example Output of Expert System (Screen #2)

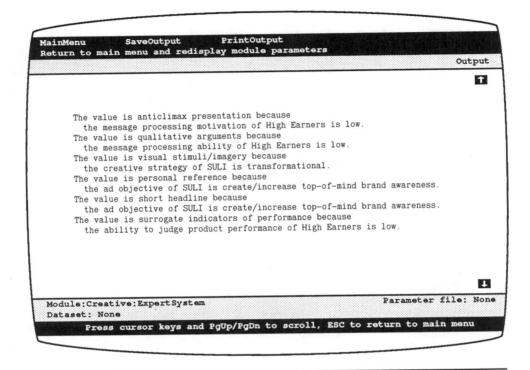

```
 MainMenu         SaveOutput        PrintOutput
 Return to main menu and redisplay module parameters
                                                           Output
                                                              ⬆

         The value is anticlimax presentation because
            the message processing motivation of High Earners is low.
         The value is qualitative arguments because
            the message processing ability of High Earners is low.
         The value is visual stimuli/imagery because
            the creative strategy of SULI is transformational.
         The value is personal reference because
            the ad objective of SULI is create/increase top-of-mind brand awareness.
         The value is short headline because
            the ad objective of SULI is create/increase top-of-mind brand awareness.
         The value is surrogate indicators of performance because
            the ability to judge product performance of High Earners is low.




                                                              ⬇
 Module:Creative:ExpertSystem                 Parameter file: None
 Dataset: None
        Press cursor keys and PgUp/PgDn to scroll, ESC to return to main menu
```

---

the Power benefit. The system has inferred that High Earners may be uninterested in the brand message, so it recommends using fantasy, exaggeration, or surrealism to attract the audience's attention.

Given the low message interest and processing ability of the target audience, ADSTRAT suggests that the key message argument be presented early in the advertisement (anticlimax format),[19] and the benefit be described in qualitative rather than quantitative terms.[20] To enhance the audience's emotional response to the transformational message, ADSTRAT recommends using visual stimuli and imagery.[21] The system also indicates that a personal reference and a short headline are useful techniques for enhancing consumers' top-of-mind recall of the SULI brand name.[22]

The user must interpret ADSTRAT's recommendations in light of his or her own knowledge of the advertising domain and the current problem. The system suggests only a few of the tremendous number of creative options available to the advertiser. Whatever creative approaches are selected, they should be relevant to the target audience and should communicate how the brand's benefit will satisfy the salient purchase motivations. If the decision maker is uncertain about the appropriate responses to the system's questions, then he or she can rerun the consultation with different input information and examine the effects on the system's recommendations.

Pitfalls to Avoid

ADSTRAT's expert system is a supplement and not a substitute for the creative process in ad design. In addition to having heuristics or rules-of-thumb, advertising creatives must understand the culture in order to select stimuli that evoke desired responses in the target audience; to portray the selling proposition in a compelling manner. For example, one advertiser used the audience's familiarity with children and cookie jars to create an ad that attracts the audience's attention and dramatizes the good taste of an alternative snack food (bananas). It would be very difficult to build this type of general knowledge into the computer system.

Another major consideration in advertising design is *ad distinctiveness*. It is estimated that consumers are exposed to between 300 and 600 ads a day (Britt, Adams, and Miller 1972). Ads must be creative and original to break through this clutter of messages and create a distinctive brand image at the point of purchase. The success of several highly original ad campaigns attests to the importance of this dimension.[23]

ADSTRAT has no mechanism for "creative thinking." The system bases its recommendations on what has been found in the past to be effective in situations with the same set of characteristics. Yet, because of its unfailing application of relevant knowledge to each new situation, ADSTRAT will often recommend options that are new to the user or that were accidentally overlooked. Perkins notes, "Far from being contrary to insight, reasoning is an important means to insight, and often a neglected one."[24] To ensure that ADSTRAT's suggestions are original, the user must screen them in light of his or her knowledge of competitive activities. If a communication approach is preempted, the user can consider other options from ADSTRAT's list of recommendations and/or vary assumptions to generate additional suggestions.

References

1. Caples, John (1975), *Tested Advertising Methods*, Englewood Cliffs, NJ: Prentice-Hall.
2. See, for example, Fishbein, Martin and Icek Ajzen (1975), *Belief, Attitude, Intention, and Behavior: An Introduction to Theory and Research*, Reading, MA: Addison-Wesley.
3. One of the most extensive studies was conducted by David W. Stewart and David H. Furse (1986), *Effective Television Advertising: A Study of 1000 Commercials*, Lexington, MA: Lexington Books.
4. Lavidge, Robert J. and Gary A. Steiner (1961), "A Model for Predictive Measurements of Advertising Effectiveness," *Journal of Marketing*, 25 (October), 59–62.
5. Krugman, Herbert E. (1965), "The Impact of Television Advertising: Learning Without Involvement," *Public Opinion Quarterly*, 29 (Fall), 349–356.
6. Petty, Richard E. and John T. Cacioppo (1983), "Central and Peripheral Routes to Persuasion: Application to Advertising," in *Advertising and Consumer Psychology*, eds. Larry Percy and Arch G. Woodside, Lexington, MA: Lexington Books, 3–23.
7. Rossiter, John R. and Larry Percy (1987), *Advertising and Promotion Management*, New York: McGraw-Hill.

8. Anand, Punam and Brian Sternthal (1986), "Strategies for Designing Persuasive Messages: Deductions from the Resource Matching Hypothesis," unpublished manuscript, New York University, April.

9. Material in this section was adapted from Burke, Raymond R., Arvind Rangaswamy, Jerry Wind, and Jehoshua Eliashberg (1990), "A Knowledge-Based System for Advertising Design," *Marketing Science*, 9 (Summer), 212–229.

10. Williams, C. Richard (1986), "The Ugliest Word in Advertising," *Advertising Age*, February 17, p.16.

11. Kingman, Merle (1981), "Who's to Blame for Sameness in Ads? Not Us: Researchers," *Advertising Age*, February 2, p.41.

12. Wells, William D. (1982), "Point of View: Let's Think While We Still Can," *Journal of Advertising Research*, 22 (February), 61–63.

13. Ogilvy, David and Joel Raphaelson (1982), "Research on Advertising Techniques that Work—and Don't Work," *Harvard Business Review*, 60 (July-August), p.16.

14. For a more complete discussion of the knowledge base and supporting citations, the reader should see Burke, Raymond R., Arvind Rangaswamy, Jerry Wind, and Jehoshua Eliashberg (1988), "ADCAD: A Knowledge-Based System for Advertising Design," Working Paper #88–027 (December), Marketing Department, The Wharton School, University of Pennsylvania.

15. Petty, Richard E. and John T. Cacioppo (1983), "Central and Peripheral Routes to Persuasion: Application to Advertising," in *Advertising and Consumer Psychology*, eds. Larry Percy and Arch G. Woodside, Lexington, MA: Lexington Books, 3–23.

16. Martilla, John A. and John C. James (1977), "Importance-Performance Analysis," *Journal of Marketing*, 41 (1), 77–79.

17. Silk, Alvin J. and Terry G. Vavra (1974), "The Influence of Advertising's Affective Qualities on Consumer Response," in *Buyer/Consumer Information Processing*, eds. G. David Hughes and Michael L. Ray, Chapel Hill, NC: University of North Carolina Press, 157–186.

18. As noted earlier, the "Escape" key will not interrupt the program's operation during the consultation period. The user must complete the consultation and wait for the system to display its recommendations before attempting to exit ADSTRAT.

19. Abelson, Herbert I. (1959), *Persuasion: How Opinions and Attitudes are Changed*, New York, NY: Springer Publishing Co.

20. Yalch, Richard F. and Rebecca Elmore-Yalch (1984), "The Effect of Numbers on the Route to Persuasion," *Journal of Consumer Research*, 11, 522–527.

21. Rossiter, John R. (1982), "Visual Imagery: Applications to Advertising," in *Advances in Consumer Research*, Vol. 9, ed. Andrew A. Mitchell, Provo, UT: Association for Consumer Research, 101–106.

22. MacLachlan, James (1984), "Making a Message Memorable and Persuasive," *Journal of Advertising Research*, 23 (January), 51–59.

23. Similar advertising can have a substantial inhibitory effect on consumers' abilities to recall advertised information. See Burke, Raymond R. and Thomas K. Srull (1988), "Competitive Interference and Consumer Memory for Advertising," *Journal of Consumer Research*, 15 (June), 55–68.

24. Perkins, D. N. (1981), *The Mind's Best Work*, Harvard University Press, p.71.

7

Media & Scheduling Decisions

Media planning is the process of designing a strategic course of action that describes how advertising space and time can be used to communicate the advertising message in order to achieve the advertiser's objectives. The goal of the media plan is to deliver the advertising message to members of the target audience in a cost-effective and impactful manner, and at a time and place when it is most likely to affect the purchase process. Toward this end, the media plan must be coordinated with the other advertising planning decisions, such as budgeting and creative strategy.

Media planning requires the advertiser to make four types of decisions:

1. *Media class decisions*—the choice of one or more channels of communication, such as television, radio, magazine, or newspaper.
2. *Media vehicle decisions*—the placement of ads in specific communication outlets, such as particular TV shows or magazines.
3. *Media option decisions*—the determination of the ad's media characteristics, such as the size, length, and color of the ad.
4. *Timing decisions*—the scheduling of media options over time. Timing depends on consumers' learning processes, as well as seasonal fluctuations in consumer demand and competitive activities.

The first decision, media class selection, is usually based on general considerations, such as the affordability of various types of media, the demographic and geographic selectivity of the media, and media communication characteristics (e.g., sight, sound, and motion).[1] The advertiser will select those media that are best suited to the particular product, message, and audience of the advertising campaign. The remaining decisions entail the allocation of the advertising budget across alternative media vehicles, options, and time periods. They are based more on quantitative considerations, and are the focus of the following discussion.

In this chapter, we present a framework for evaluating media planning decisions, and then describe ADSTRAT's tools for allocating the advertising budget across media alternatives. Before continuing this discussion, it would be helpful to define a few additional terms that are commonly used in the media planning area:

Ad insertion:	The placement of a single advertisement in a specific media vehicle and option at a certain point in time.
Exposure:	Whether an individual has "seen" the advertisement. Note that exposure does not necessarily imply audience processing of the advertised information.
Audience:	The number of people or households who are exposed to a media vehicle. This exposure constitutes an opportunity for audience members to be exposed to advertisements placed in the medium.
Frequency:	The number of times an audience is exposed to the advertisement over a certain time period.
Reach:	The number of different people who are exposed to a particular media vehicle at least once during a certain time period.
Effective reach:	The percentage of a vehicle's audience that belongs to the target market. For example, if a media vehicle has a 50 percent effective reach, half of the audience consists of members of the target segment.
Coverage:	The fraction of people in a target market who are in the audience of a given vehicle. For example, if a media vehicle has a 50 percent coverage, half of the target segment is a member of the vehicle's audience.

A Framework for Evaluating Media Allocation Decisions

The decisions about where and how often to advertise are complex, and depend on a number of factors. Figure 7.1 presents a conceptual framework for evaluating media allocation decisions. The box in the upper right-hand corner represents the objectives or criteria used to evaluate the quality of the media plan. These should correspond to the advertiser's communication objectives, as discussed in Chapter 4. The bottom-line objective of most advertising campaigns is to increase sales, market share, or profits, so these variables are often used to track media performance. However, advertisers also use measures of the various stages of the hierarchy of effects as criteria. One might argue, for example, that the media plan should be designed to maximize advertising exposures to the target audience because ad exposure is a necessary condition for producing any further consumer response.

In the upper left-hand corner of Figure 7.1, we list a number of factors that affect how consumers will react to advertising and should be considered in the

Figure 7.1

A Conceptual Framework for Evaluating Media Allocation Decisions

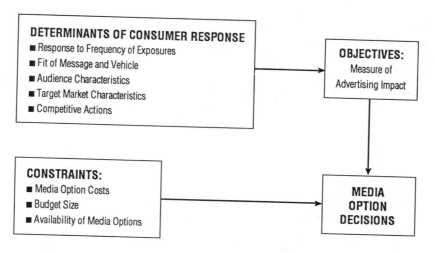

media planning decision. The first is *frequency of exposure*. As discussed in Chapter 5, an audience's response to an ad depends on the number of times the audience has seen, heard, or read the ad in the past, the recency of past exposure, and its prior knowledge of the advertised brand. Another important factor is the *fit of the media vehicle* with the ad's message. In general, customers will have a greater response to an ad if it is placed in a vehicle with a positive image (i.e., high prestige, expertise, objectivity), high reproduction quality (in print, e.g., large page size, high paper quality, color), and compatible programming or editorial content.

A third major consideration is the vehicle's *audience characteristics*. Media alternatives vary in the size and composition of their audiences, and in the level of audience involvement. Holding other factors constant, the advertiser would prefer to place ads in vehicles that reach the largest percentage of the target segment and generate the highest levels of consumer interest. The fourth factor is the *target market characteristics*. Target segments differ in size, propensity to purchase the product, and patterns of purchasing over time. The advertiser often places more emphasis on reaching the largest and most profitable segments. Finally, *competitors' advertising* and other marketing activities should be considered, as they can affect consumer response.

The box in the lower left of Figure 7.1 represents another set of factors that impact the budget allocation decision. However, these factors are different from the list above in that they operate as constraints on media selection. The *cost* of placing an ad in each vehicle and the *size of the media budget* will affect the choice of vehicles and limit the number of ad insertions. There are also constraints on

---

Figure 7.2

Factors Considered in Media Efficiency Option

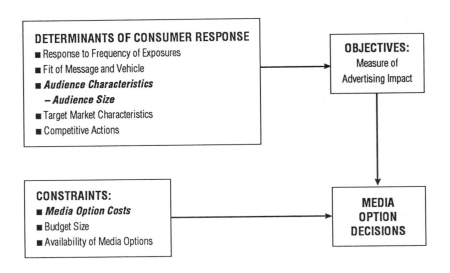

the *availability* of media space and time. For example, advertisers typically will not place more than one ad in an issue of a magazine. For monthly periodicals, this limits the number of possible ad insertions in a given magazine to 12 per year. Some media will also give category exclusivity to an advertiser during certain time periods, thus preempting other advertisers.

ADSTRAT offers several analysis tools for media planning, from simple media selection approaches based on audience size and cost to more sophisticated model-based approaches which represent how consumers respond to repeated advertising exposures over time. With the "Efficiency" option, the user can examine the cost per thousand performance of a number of media alternatives. Next, he or she can apply the "Allocation" option (a linear programming approach[2]) to vehicle exposure data, costs, and subjective estimates of vehicle/option source effects in order to allocate the advertising budget across media vehicles. Finally, ADSTRAT provides a media planning model based on the MEDIAC model.[3] This "MediaAid" option allows the user to develop a media plan in the context of a more realistic model of consumer response to advertising. This model can be used either to simulate the response of consumers to a particular insertion schedule or to select an "optimal" insertion schedule under a user-specified budget constraint.

The media planning options in ADSTRAT cover many of the factors presented in Figure 7.1. In general, as the number of factors considered increases, so does the complexity of the analysis procedure and the amount of information required. As we describe each of the tools in the following sections, we will evaluate them in terms of this framework.

─────────────────────── Figure 7.3 ───────────────────────

Media Decision Options

```
  Efficiency   Allocation   MediaAid
  Media efficiency: Cost Per Thousand
                                                          Module




















  Module:Media                              Parameter file: None
  Dataset: None
  Select the option to be used
```

Media Efficiency

The standard measure of media efficiency is the "cost per thousand" (CPM) figure. This measure is simply the cost of inserting an ad in a vehicle (in dollars) divided by the size of the vehicle's audience (in thousands of people). It represents the cost of reaching one thousand people one time. The lower the CPM, the higher the efficiency of the vehicle. Figure 7.2 illustrates the subset of factors considered when using CPM estimates for media planning.

The cost and audience size data for calculating CPMs are supplied by media representatives and various research companies.[4] The cost figures vary depending on the total amount of vehicle time or space purchased by the advertiser, and on the specific media options chosen. Audience figures vary depending on whether they are based on the total population or a specific market segment, and, in the case of print, on whether estimates indicate circulation (copies sold) or actual readership (including pass-along readership).

ADSTRAT's media dataset provides information on the cost of inserting a single ad in various media vehicles and options. As discussed in Chapter 2, the cost figures represent the costs of placing full-page magazine ads, quarter-page newspaper ads, or 30 second TV commercials, as the case may be. ADSTRAT's audience size figures reflect the total number of people who see, hear, or read

---

Figure 7.4

Selection of Vehicles for Media Efficiency Option

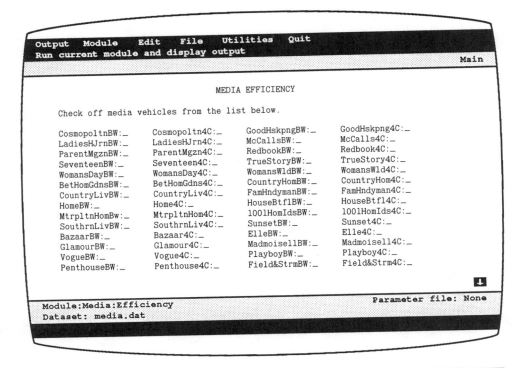

the media vehicles on an average occasion. The figures do not indicate the vehicles' abilities to reach a particular market segment. Therefore, the CPM information should only be used as first-cut in screening alternatives, and to compare options that have similar appeal to the target audience.

Selecting the Efficiency Option

The cost per thousand module is accessed by selecting "Module" from the main menu, and then selecting "Media." Three options are displayed: Efficiency, Allocation, and MediaAid (Figure 7.3). The user should choose the first menu item (Efficiency). The system displays the first page of the input template, which lists the vehicles and options in the media dataset (Figure 7.4).[5] To pick alternatives for analysis, the user should select "Edit" from the main menu, and the cursor will move to the template area.

Selecting Vehicles and Options

The user can scan through the available media vehicles by pressing the "Page Up" and "Page Down" keys on the computer's cursor control pad. A vehicle name may appear several times with different suffixes, representing multiple

---

Figure 7.5

Example of Selection of Vehicles for Media Efficiency Option

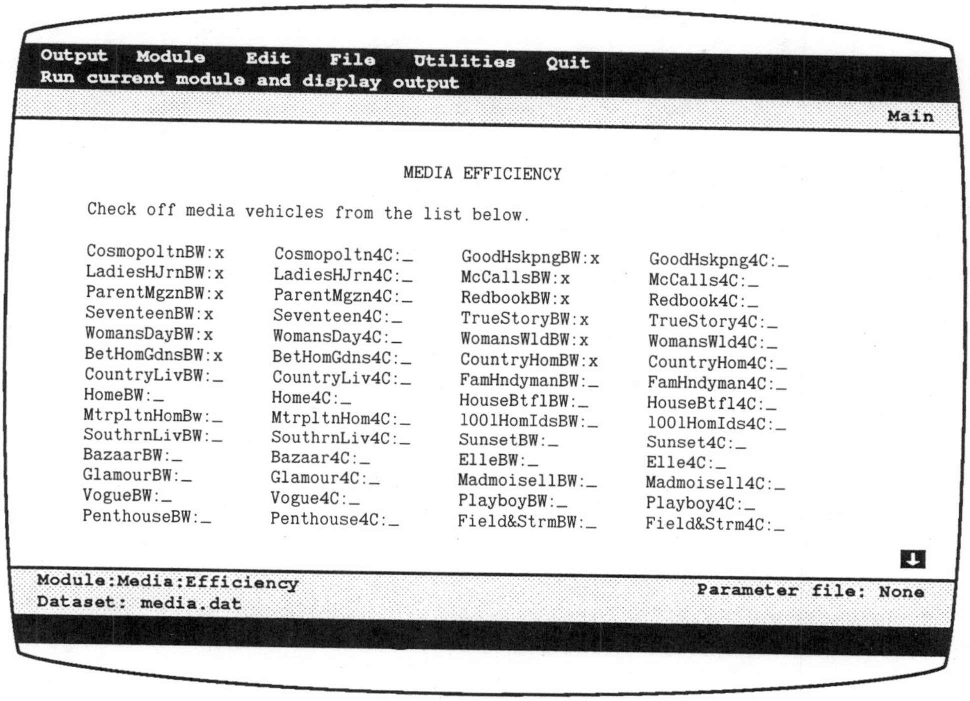

```
 Output   Module   Edit   File   Utilities   Quit
 Run current module and display output

                                                        Main

                       MEDIA EFFICIENCY

   Check off media vehicles from the list below.

   CosmopoltnBW:x    Cosmopoltn4C:_    GoodHskpngBW:x    GoodHskpng4C:_
   LadiesHJrnBW:x    LadiesHJrn4C:_    McCallsBW:x       McCalls4C:_
   ParentMgznBW:x    ParentMgzn4C:_    RedbookBW:x       Redbook4C:_
   SeventeenBW:x     Seventeen4C:_     TrueStoryBW:x     TrueStory4C:_
   WomansDayBW:x     WomansDay4C:_     WomansWldBW:x     WomansWld4C:_
   BetHomGdnsBW:x    BetHomGdns4C:_    CountryHomBW:x    CountryHom4C:_
   CountryLivBW:_    CountryLiv4C:_    FamHndymanBW:_    FamHndyman4C:_
   HomeBW:_          Home4C:_          HouseBtflBW:_     HouseBtfl4C:_
   MtrpltnHomBw:_    MtrpltnHom4C:_    1001HomIdsBW:_    1001HomIds4C:_
   SouthrnLivBW:_    SouthrnLiv4C:_    SunsetBW:_        Sunset4C:_
   BazaarBW:_        Bazaar4C:_        ElleBW:_          Elle4C:_
   GlamourBW:_       Glamour4C:_       MadmoisellBW:_    Madmoisell4C:_
   VogueBW:_         Vogue4C:_         PlayboyBW:_       Playboy4C:_
   PenthouseBW:_     Penthouse4C:_     Field&StrmBW:_    Field&Strm4C:_
                                                            ⬇

 Module:Media:Efficiency                     Parameter file: None
 Dataset: media.dat
```

---

options. For example, magazines are listed with both black and white (BW) and four-color (4C) options. While in edit mode, the user can select a vehicle/option by moving the cursor to the corresponding check box and pressing the "space bar." Any number of alternatives can be checked at a time. In Figure 7.5, the user has asked the system to report CPM figures for full-page black-and-white print ads in 12 different women's and home service magazines. To run the cost per thousand analysis, the user should "Escape" from edit mode, and then select the "Output" option.

The Efficiency Output

An example of the module's output is displayed in Figure 7.6. The output lists the size of the audience (in thousands), the cost of an insertion (in dollars), and the cost per thousand ratio for each of the selected alternatives. In this example, it appears that *Woman's World* magazine is the most efficient vehicle for reaching people, with a CPM of $8.68. One of the reasons for its low cost is that it is published weekly whereas the other periodicals are published monthly. *Country Home* is the most expensive alternative on a cost per thousand basis, due in part to its high print quality and upscale audience.

Figure 7.6

Example Output of Media Efficiency Option

```
MainMenu        SaveOutput        PrintOutput
Return to main menu and redisplay module parameters
                                                              Output
                                                                 ⬆

                          MEDIA EFFICIENCY

    Vehicle Option    Audience Size   Cost/Insertion   Cost/Thousand
                         (000)             ($)             ($)

    ---------------   -------------   --------------   -------------
    CosmopoltnBW          2935            32170            10.96
    GoodHskpngBW          5142            66965            13.02
    LadiesHJrnBW          5121            52300            10.21
    McCallsBW             5275            51400             9.74
    ParentMgznBW          1729            29870            17.28
    RedbookBW             3891            43875            11.28
    SeventeenBW           1804            21100            11.70
    TrueStoryBW           1444            13355             9.25
    WomansDayBW           5632            53465             9.49
    WomansWldBW           1337            11600             8.68
    BetHomGdnsBW          8012            82025            10.24
    CountryHomBW           811            18700            23.06

                                                                 ⬇
Module:Media:Efficiency                      Parameter file: None
Dataset: media.dat
    Press cursor keys and PgUp/PgDn to scroll, ESC to return to main menu
```

The user should be cautious when comparing cost per thousand figures across media because of the substantial differences in the quality of the exposure. For example, a 30 second television commercial can communicate sound and motion, whereas a magazine ad has higher quality reproduction and a greater degree of permanence. CPM figures are most useful for making within-medium comparisons.

Evaluation of the Media Efficiency Option

The CPM ratio is an indicator of the efficiency of a vehicle in reaching the total population. It assumes that all individuals in the audience have the same value to the advertiser. CPM figures must be adjusted in cases where the advertiser is attempting to reach a defined target audience or segment. In addition, they should be modified to reflect the degree of fit between the advertising message and the editorial climate of the various vehicles. These issues will be addressed in the next section describing the linear programming approach to media allocation.

The cost-per-thousand method is a simple analysis which uses readily available media information. It allows the decision maker to rank the media options on cost, audience size, and overall efficiency, and to screen out alternatives that are clearly inconsistent with the advertising objectives. However, it neglects most of the important factors identified in Figure 7.3. To evaluate these factors, the advertiser will need additional media and consumer information. It should also be noted that the cost-per-thousand method does not allocate the ad budget across alternatives or indicate the performance of a particular media plan. These issues are addressed by various media planning models, two of which are discussed in the remainder of this chapter.

Media Allocation: Linear Programming

Media planning models attempt to select the best media schedule given a budget constraint and information about the vehicles under consideration.[6] Mathematical programming formulations of the media selection problem became popular early in the development of planning models. These approaches seek to find an optimal distribution of ad insertions across media vehicles such that an "objective function" (which estimates effective reach, sales, or profits, for example) is maximized.

ADSTRAT's "Allocation" option applies a linear programming approach to the media planning problem.[7] This approach is an improvement over the CPM method in that it incorporates several of the moderating factors discussed earlier in the chapter (see Figure 7.7). Specifically, the Allocation option adjusts the estimated audience size of each media vehicle/option to reflect: (1) its ability to reach members of the target segment (effective reach), (2) consumers' relative interest in the vehicle's advertising (ad exposure probability), and (3) its effectiveness at communicating the ad message (option effect). The linear programming method allocates the total media budget across media vehicles and options, and indicates the number of ads to place in each alternative.

Problem Formulation

The linear programming method assumes that the media planning objective is to maximize the number of "effective" (or weighted) ad exposures to individuals in the target audience, given a defined budget and certain other constraints. To simplify the discussion, let us first consider unweighted or "raw" exposures. One can estimate the total number of ad exposures produced by a given media schedule by multiplying the audience size of each vehicle by the number of insertions in that vehicle, and summing across vehicles. The objective function would then be:

$$\text{Maximize} \sum_{j=1}^{N} r_j x_j \tag{7.1}$$

where:

r_j = number of individuals reached by vehicle j (audience size),
x_j = number of insertions in vehicle j,
N = total number of vehicles.

Figure 7.7

Factors Considered in Media Allocation Option

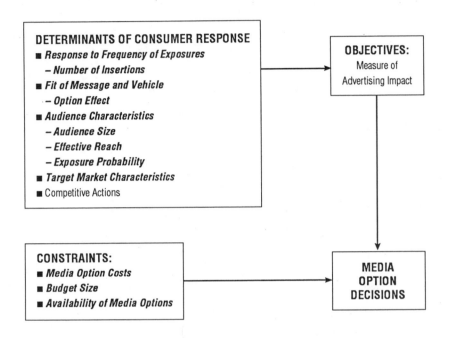

This calculation of total exposures represents some combination of the reach and frequency of the media plan. The levels of reach and frequency obtained are determined by the degree of "internal" and "external overlap" in the composition of audiences across time and vehicles. If the media plan places multiple ad insertions in one vehicle and the audience reads this publication or views this program on a regular basis (high internal overlap), then the same individuals are likely to be exposed to the ad several times. On the other hand, if the plan inserts ads in a variety of different vehicles, and different individuals view or read these alternatives (low external overlap), then ad exposure frequency is likely to be low.[8] The linear programming method ignores these distinctions, placing equal weight on exposures that increase reach and frequency.

There are a number of constraints on the volume of advertising. The first is the advertising budget. The budget must be greater than or equal to the total cost of the insertions across vehicles. One must also consider institutional constraints on the number of insertions for each vehicle. As noted earlier, advertisers typically place only one ad insertion in a single issue of a magazine. Therefore, a monthly magazine could have a maximum of twelve insertions per year. The advertiser may also specify the minimum number of insertions per vehicle. This value is usually set to zero (no constraint). However, in some cases, it might be desirable to force the model to place a certain number of ads in a vehicle.

The problem as stated above is merely a formalization of the cost per thousand method. The linear programming model automatically ranks the alternatives and places ads in the most efficient vehicles subject the budget and other constraints. To address the exposure quality, ad attention, and segmentation issues discussed above, we introduce three indices into the model. The effective reach index indicates the percentage of the vehicle's audience that belongs to the target audience. The exposure probability index represents the audience's likelihood of being exposed to an ad given that it is exposed to the vehicle. The option source effect index indicates the quality of the exposure, or the degree of match between the ad message and the image of the vehicle. The advertiser estimates these index values (on a scale from zero to one) for each vehicle and option using media research, copy testing results, and subjective judgment. To calculate the number of "effective" exposures per vehicle, the linear programming model multiplies the "raw" exposures per vehicle by the three vehicle effectiveness indices.

Selecting the Allocation Option

The media allocation module is accessed by selecting "Module" from the main menu, and then selecting "Media" and "Allocation." The system displays the first page of the input template, which lists a set of media vehicles/options and the default index values (Figure 7.8). To identify alternatives and enter information, the user should select "Edit" from the main menu, and the cursor will move to the template area (edit mode).

Defining Problem Parameters

The first decision concerns the size of the advertising budget to allocate. This value should be based on the budgeting analyses discussed in Chapter 5. The budget figure can be easily varied to observe its effect on the model's recommendations. In the example shown in Figure 7.9, the value of $2,000,000 is entered.

The user can then select a set of vehicles and options by moving the cursor to the corresponding check boxes and pressing the "space bar." Any number of alternatives can be checked at a time. In theory, the user could select all of the possible options, since the methodology will reject ineffective alternatives by recommending zero insertions. However, given the limitations on computer memory and processing time, the user should first attempt to eliminate some options based on cost, audience, and message-fit considerations. The cost and audience size information can be obtained from the media efficiency module.

The user can then enter the minimum and maximum numbers of insertions for each vehicle of interest. The default values are 0 and 12, which would be appropriate for monthly publications and a one-year planning period. These figures will need to be changed for newspapers, television programs, and weekly magazines. The user may consider setting lower maximum values in cases where the actual values (e.g., 52 issues per year) may produce unnecessarily high levels of ad exposure.

—————————————— Figure 7.8 ——————————————

Default Values for Media Allocation Option

```
                                                                    Edit

                        MEDIA ALLOCATION

    Budget:_____

    Check off media vehicles from the list below.

                      Exposure  Effective  Option
                        Prob.     Reach     Effect    Min   Max
       CosmopoltnBW:_    :1.00     :1.00     :1.00    :  0  : 12
       Cosmopoltn4C:_    :1.00     :1.00     :1.00    :  0  : 12
       GoodHskpngBW:_    :1.00     :1.00     :1.00    :  0  : 12
       GoodHskpng4C:_    :1.00     :1.00     :1.00    :· 0  : 12
       LadiesHJrnBW:_    :1.00     :1.00     :1.00    :  0  : 12
       LadiesHJrn4C:_    :1.00     :1.00     :1.00    :  0  : 12
          McCallsBW:_    :1.00     :1.00     :1.00    :  0  : 12
          McCalls4C:_    :1.00     :1.00     :1.00    :  0  : 12
       ParentMgznBW:_    :1.00     :1.00     :1.00    :  0  : 12
       ParentMgzn4C:_    :1.00     :1.00     :1.00    :  0  : 12
                                                                     ⬇

    Module:Media:Allocation                     Parameter file: None
    Dataset: media.dat
    Press cursor keys to move, PgUp/PgDn to scroll, ESC to return to main menu
```

Finally, the decision maker can input the index values for each of the selected vehicles and options. The exposure probability, effective reach, and option source effects have default values of 1.0. These values assume that audience members are exposed to every ad in each vehicle, that the entire audience of each vehicle is in the target segment, and that there are no differences between vehicles and options in their effectiveness for communicating the ad message. If the analysis is run with these default values, then the model will allocate the budget across media vehicle options on a purely cost-per-thousand basis.

Information on the effective reach of the media alternatives can be obtained through analyses of the survey dataset (see Chapter 3). This file includes data on the media habits of survey respondents. By crosstabulating the segmentation criterion (or cluster group) with magazine readership or television viewing, the user can derive estimates of the proportion of the vehicle's audience that consists of members of the target segment.[9] If the user finds that 15 percent of Cosmopolitan readers are in the target audience, then he or she would enter 0.15 as the effective reach for that alternative (Figure 7.9).

Figure 7.9 provides an example where a number of magazines have been selected and effective reach information has been entered.[10] (Only the first page

─────────────── Figure 7.9 ───────────────

Example of Basic Input for Media Allocation Option

```
                                                        Edit

                        MEDIA ALLOCATION

        Budget:2000000.00

        Check off media vehicles from the list below.

                        Exposure  Effective  Option
                          Prob.     Reach     Effect    Min   Max
        CosmopoltnBW:x    :1.00     :0.15     :1.00     :  0  : 12
        Cosmopoltn4C:x    :1.00     :0.15     :1.00     :  0  : 12
        GoodHskpngBW:_    :1.00     :1.00     :1.00     :  0  : 12
        GoodHskpng4C:x    :1.00     :0.42     :1.00     :  0  : 12
        LadiesHJrnBW:_    :1.00     :1.00     :1.00     :  0  : 12
        LadiesHJrn4C:x    :1.00     :0.37     :1.00     :  0  : 12
          McCallsBW:_     :1.00     :1.00     :1.00     :  0  : 12
          McCalls4C:x     :1.00     :0.50     :1.00     :  0  : 12
        ParentMgznBW:_    :1.00     :1.00     :1.00     :  0  : 12
        ParentMgzn4C:_    :1.00     :1.00     :1.00     :  0  : 12

                                                             ⬇

 Module:Media:Allocation                    Parameter file: None
 Dataset: media.dat
   Press cursor keys to move, PgUp/PgDn to scroll, ESC to return to main menu
```

of the template is shown.) In this example, exposure probabilities and option source effects are assumed to be the same for all options (1.00). Therefore, when allocating the budget, the linear programming model only adjusts the audience size figures for the segmentation effect. The analysis results are presented in Figure 7.10 and discussed in the next section.

The remaining parameters (the exposure probabilities and option source effects) are more subjective.[11] The user sets these values to reflect differences in the effectiveness of media vehicle options. As noted earlier, the exposure probability factor represents the likelihood that someone in the target population who is exposed to the media option will also be exposed to the ad. It is likely to be higher (closer to 1.00) for large or long ads placed in media with high audience interest and low advertising clutter. The option source effect is the quality of the exposure given that the audience member has seen the ad. It will be higher for options that are better at communicating the advertising message and the brand's personality. For example, an ad for perfume might benefit from being placed in a television soap opera with romantic content. Figure 7.11 illustrates possible input for the option source effect. In this example, the user has assumed that a color ad in Cosmopolitan will have three times the impact of a black-and-white ad on the target audience.

─────────── Figure 7.10 ───────────

Example Output of Media Allocation Option

```
┌─────────────────────────────────────────────────────────────────────────┐
│ MainMenu        SaveOutput        PrintOutput                             │
│ Return to main menu and redisplay module parameters                      │
│                                                                  Output   │
│                                                                           │
│                         MEDIA ALLOCATION                                  │
│                                                                           │
│                                       Effective Overall                   │
│   Media        No.   Boundaries      exposure vehicle  Exp.  Eff. Option  │
│   name         ins   min  max   Cost  [000]    effect  prob. Rch. effect  │
│  ----------    ----  ---------  ----- -------- ------                     │
│                                                                           │
│  ----  ----  -----                                                        │
│  CosmopoltnBW    1    0   12    32170     440    0.15   1.00  0.15  1.00   │
│  Cosmopoltn4C    0    0   12        0       0    0.15   1.00  0.15  1.00   │
│  GoodHskpng4C    0    0   12        0       0    0.42   1.00  0.42  1.00   │
│  LadiesHJrn4C    0    0   12        0       0    0.37   1.00  0.37  1.00   │
│  McCalls4C      12    0   12   759600   31650    0.50   1.00  0.50  1.00   │
│  BetHomGdns4C   12    0   12  1190580   46149    0.48   1.00  0.48  1.00   │
│  Bazaar4C        0    0   12        0       0    0.13   1.00  0.13  1.00   │
│  Elle4C          0    0   12        0       0    0.29   1.00  0.29  1.00   │
│                                                                           │
│  Total used: 1982350  of budget: 2000000                                 │
│  99.1 % of budget used                                                    │
│     78239 total effective exposure                                        │
│                                                                           │
│ Module:Media:Efficiency                          Parameter file: None     │
│ Dataset: media.dat                                                        │
│      Press cursor keys and PgUp/PgDn to scroll, ESC to return to main menu │
└─────────────────────────────────────────────────────────────────────────┘
```

The Media Allocation Output

Figures 7.10 and 7.12 display the linear programming output for the two sets of parameters described above. For each of the media options selected, the system lists the number of recommended ad insertions, the total ad expenditures, and the estimated number of effective exposures. The remaining columns summarize the user's input to the model. The "overall vehicle effect" is the product of the three components: exposure probability, effective reach, and option effect.

Comparing the two analyses, one can see that the system initially schedules 12 insertions in *McCalls* (Figure 7.10), but then shifts these advertising dollars to *Ladies Home Journal* (Figure 7.12) as a result of the second vehicle's higher estimated impact. ADSTRAT also makes the initial suggestion of placing a black-and-white ad in *Cosmopolitan*. However, when the user indicates that the absence of color would substantially reduce the ad's effectiveness, the system recommends other alternatives.

At the end of the output, ADSTRAT reports the amount and proportion of the budget allocated, and the total effective exposures generated by the media plan. The reader should note that this exposure estimate depends on the values of the three indices. While the first two parameters (exposure probability and effective

--- Figure 7.11 ---

Example of Vehicle Option Effects for Media Allocation Option

```
                                                                    Edit

                          MEDIA ALLOCATION

        Budget:2000000.00

        Check off media vehicles from the list below.

                      Exposure  Effective  Option
                        Prob.     Reach     Effect    Min   Max
        CosmopoltnBW:x   :1.00    :0.15     :0.30    :  0  : 12
        Cosmopoltn4C:x   :1.00    :0.15     :0.90    :  0  : 12
        GoodHskpngBW:_   :1.00    :1.00     :1.00    :  0  : 12
        GoodHskpng4C:x   :1.00    :0.42     :0.50    :  0  : 12
        LadiesHJrnBW:_   :1.00    :1.00     :1.00    :  0  : 12
        LadiesHJrn4C:x   :1.00    :0.37     :0.45    :  0  : 12
          McCallsBW:_    :1.00    :1.00     :1.00    :  0  : 12
          McCalls4C:x    :1.00    :0.50     :0.30    :  0  : 12
        ParentMgznBW:_   :1.00    :1.00     :1.00    :  0  : 12
        ParentMgzn4C:_   :1.00    :1.00     :1.00    :  0  : 12
                                                              ⬇

  Module:Media:Allocation
  Dataset: media.dat                       Parameter file: None
  Press cursor keys to move, PgUp/PgDn to scroll, ESC to return to main menu
```

reach) are meaningful in absolute terms, the option source effect only represents the relative value of one option compared to another. Therefore, the user should not select one media plan over another based on these exposure estimates when the option effect indices vary across plans.[12]

Evaluation of the Media Allocation Option

The media allocation module is easy to apply and can take into consideration a number of factors that are elementary to the vehicle choice problem. There are, however, a number of limitations. The first problem is that this approach assumes a linear response function. However, there is general agreement that there are eventually decreasing returns for increased advertising spending. At some point, all consumers in the target audience will be exposed to the message and will have received the information. There may also be an initial threshold in consumers' response to advertising; i.e., at low levels of advertising, increases in exposure frequency are increasingly effective up to some point, after which there are diminishing returns.[13] A threshold may exist because consumers need to be exposed to an ad a certain number of times before they pay attention to it, comprehend it, agree with it, recall it, and/or purchase the advertised brand.

--- Figure 7.12 ---

Example Output of Media Allocation Option

```
┌──────────────────────────────────────────────────────────────────────────┐
│ MainMenu        SaveOutput        PrintOutput                              │
│ Return to main menu and redisplay module parameters                       │
│                                                                   Output   │
│                                                                            │
│                         MEDIA ALLOCATION                                   │
│                                                                            │
│                                   Effective Overall                        │
│  Media        No.   Boundaries          exposure vehicle  Exp.  Eff. Option│
│  name         ins   min  max   Cost       [000]   effect  prob. Rch. effect│
│  ──────────   ────  ───  ───  ────────  ────────  ──────  ────  ──── ──────│
│  CosmopoltnBW   0    0   12        0        0       0.05   1.00  0.15  0.30 │
│  Cosmopoltn4C   0    0   12        0        0       0.14   1.00  0.15  0.90 │
│  GoodHskpng4C   0    0   12        0        0       0.21   1.00  0.42  0.50 │
│  LadiesHJrn4C  12    0   12   771600    10232       0.17   1.00  0.37  0.40 │
│  McCalls4C      0    0   12        0        0       0.15   1.00  0.50  0.30 │
│  BetHomGdns4C  12    0   12  1190580    18460       0.19   1.00  0.48  0.40 │
│  Bazaar4C       0    0   12        0        0       0.09   1.00  0.13  0.70 │
│  Elle4C         1    0   12    18982      110       0.23   1.00  0.29  0.80 │
│                                                                            │
│  Total used: 1981162  of budget: 2000000                                   │
│  99.1 % of budget used                                                     │
│     28801 total effective exposure                                         │
│                                                                            │
│ Module:Media:Efficiency                          Parameter file: None      │
│ Dataset: media.dat                                                         │
│  Press cursor keys and PgUp/PgDn to scroll, ESC to return to main menu     │
└──────────────────────────────────────────────────────────────────────────┘
```

There are a number of other concerns with this approach. The model assumes a linear cost function; that is, that the cost per ad insertion does not depend on the quantity of space or time purchased in a given vehicle. In practice, there are usually quantity discounts. The model does not provide guidance for how advertising should be scheduled over time. Finally, this approach does not consider differences in sales potential across market segments.

To address these issues, a media planning model requires flexibility in the shape of its response function, a representation of the dynamics of consumer demand, learning, and forgetting, and information on the sales potential of the various market segments. These factors are incorporated in the media aid module described in the next section. Because of the increased complexity and information demands of this approach, the user may find it useful to conduct a preliminary analysis of alternatives with the efficiency and allocation methods to select a set of candidate vehicles, and then apply the media aid module to this set to develop a final schedule.

Media Aid: A Decision Aid Model

ADSTRAT's media aid module is based on the MEDIAC model developed by Little

─────── Figure 7.13 ───────

Factors Considered in Media Aid Option

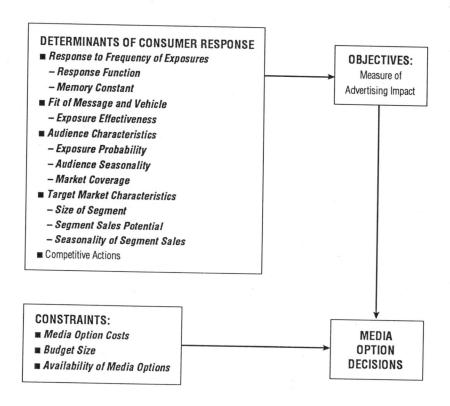

and Lodish.[14] Like the budget aid option discussed in Chapter 5, this is a decision calculus model which incorporates both objective (media cost and coverage) and subjective (audience response and media effectiveness) information.

The MEDIAC model captures most of the important media planning factors discussed at the beginning of the chapter, as shown in Figure 7.13. Audience response to the frequency of ad exposures is represented by a flexible response function which includes both learning and forgetting components. The fit of the message with the media options is represented by an index of exposure effectiveness. Three audience dimensions are considered: audience size (adjusted for seasonal variations), effective reach, and ad exposure probability. The model also represents target market characteristics, including the size and sales potential of the various market segments (adjusted for seasonal changes). The only moderating variable which is not explicitly specified in this module is competitive actions (e.g., competitive advertising). However, the user can implicitly consider competitors' activities when specifying the response function. The model also considers the various constraints on the selection of media options shown at the bottom-left of Figure 7.13.

This model can be used in two, complementary ways. The user can propose a certain media schedule and then perform a simulation to predict the sales for each market segment. Alternatively, the model can search for the best possible allocation of the advertising budget across vehicles and time periods to maximize sales. In this mode, ADSTRAT recommends the number of ad insertions to place in each media option and time period. In either case, the user must critically evaluate the model's output in light of the assumptions made in using the model. Little describes how a manager might interact with a media scheduling model:

> The first step in using the model is preparing the input data. This requires a fair amount of reflection about the problem at hand, a certain effort spent digging out numbers, and usually subjective estimates of several quantities. Thereafter, the model is run and a schedule is generated.
>
> The user looks at the schedule and immediately starts to consider whether it makes sense to him or not. Is it about what he expected? Sometimes it is and, if so, usually that is that. Oftentimes, however, the schedule does not quite agree with his intuition. It may even differ substantially. Then he wants to know why. A process starts of finding out what it was about the inputs that made the outputs come out as they did. This usually can be discovered without too much difficulty by a combination of inspection, consideration of how the model works, and various sensitivity analyses.
>
> . . .
>
> The whole process might be described as an updating of his intuition. The model has served the function of interrelating a number of factors and, in this case, not all the implications of the interrelations were evident to him when he started.[15] [p. 468–469]

In the remainder of this chapter, we discuss the MEDIAC model and then describe the operation of ADSTRAT's media aid module.

A Model of Advertising Effects on Sales

The MEDIAC model makes the following general assumptions: The population of consumers can be divided into a number of distinct market segments. Individuals in each segment have their own sales potential and media habits. When advertisements are placed in media options, a certain number of people in each segment are exposed to the advertising. These exposures build up the audience's knowledge of (and preference for) the product over time. However, in the absence of advertising, this knowledge is eventually forgotten. The sales response of customers in each market segment increases with increasing levels of exposure according to a response function. The reader can think of the process in terms of a hierarchy of effects framework, where ad exposure leads first to knowledge and preference, and then to purchase behavior.

The first step in modeling this process is to identify the determinants of ad exposure. We can define d_{sjt} as an aggregate measure of the "exposure efficiency" of media option j for a target market or segment s. This term can be thought of as the probability that an individual in segment s will be exposed to an ad if it is placed in vehicle j in time period t. This value depends on the coverage of segment s by media option j, the probability of ad exposure given that an individual is in the audience of media option j, and seasonal fluctuations in audience size in time period t. The exposure efficiency measure can be expressed as:

$$d_{sjt} = h_j g_{sj} k_{jt}$$

(7.2)

where:

h_j = the probability of exposure to a particular ad given that an individual is in the audience of media option j,

g_{sj} = market coverage; i.e., the fraction of people in segment s who are in the audience of media option j,

k_{jt} = seasonality index of market coverage (averages 1.0).

In order to facilitate comparisons across ADSTRAT's media options, we define market coverage in terms of the effective reach and audience size concepts introduced in the discussion of the media efficiency and allocation modules. An option's market coverage is equal to (effective reach × audience size)/total segment size. The media aid module takes the effective reach information as input, and combines it with audience and segment size data to calculate market coverage.

The next step is to represent how consumers "learn" or are affected by multiple ad exposures over time. The degree of consumer learning, or "exposure value," at time period t depends on the current level of advertising and its effectiveness, as well as what has been learned in the past (period $t - 1$). Of course, memory is not perfect, so some level of advertising is necessary to maintain customers' knowledge of the brand over time. The equation for calculating exposure value is:

$$y_{s,t} = \alpha y_{s,t-1} + \sum_{j=1}^{N} d_{sjt} \, e_j x_{jt}$$

(7.3)

where:

y_{st} = exposure value in segment s at period t,

α = memory constant,

e_j = media option source effect,

x_{jt} = number of insertions in media option j at time t.

The product of the exposure efficiency and the media option source effect constitutes the impact of a single ad insertion in media option j at time t on segment s's exposure value. These impact values are multiplied by the number of insertions in each media option, and then summed across media options to calculate the incremental effects of advertising at period t. Presumably, some fraction, α, of the exposure value produced by past advertising carries over to the present period. The α parameter represents the degree of memory or retention of past values. The current exposure value is simply the addition of the carryover effects of past advertising plus the effects of current advertising.

Figure 7.14

Editing the Media Aid Option

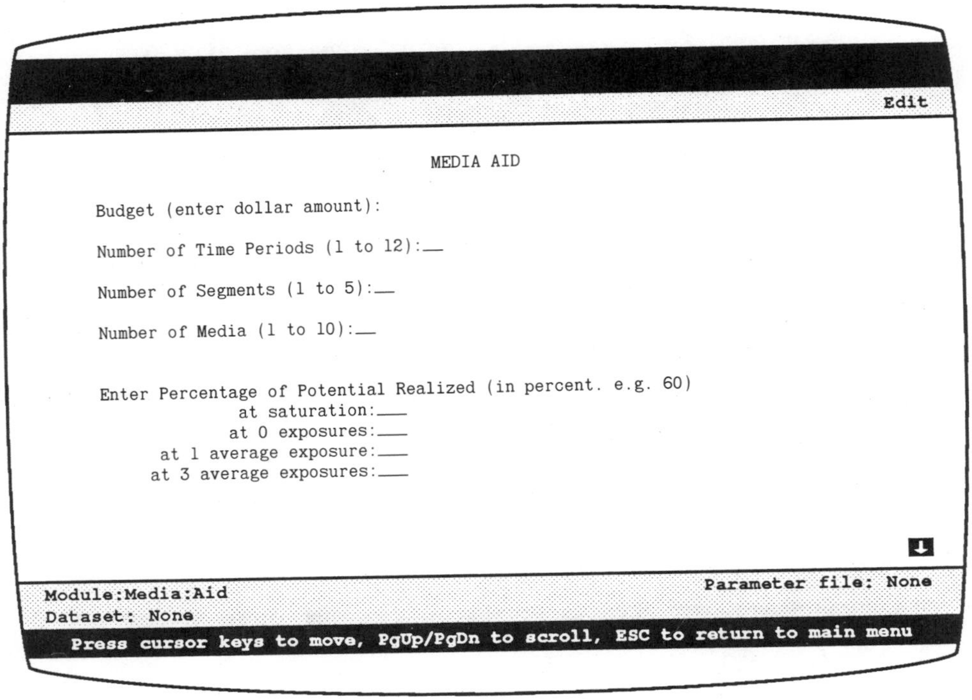

```
                                                                  Edit

                             MEDIA AID

   Budget (enter dollar amount):

   Number of Time Periods (1 to 12):__

   Number of Segments (1 to 5):__

   Number of Media (1 to 10):__


   Enter Percentage of Potential Realized (in percent. e.g. 60)
                    at saturation:__
                    at 0 exposures:__
              at 1 average exposure:__
             at 3 average exposures:__


                                                                    ⬇

   Module:Media:Aid                               Parameter file: None
   Dataset: None
   Press cursor keys to move, PgUp/PgDn to scroll, ESC to return to main menu
```

The model further assumes that a market segment's sales response in period t is determined by its accumulated exposure value in that period. As noted earlier, it is likely that the sales response function is not linear. As the cumulative exposure value in segment s at time t increases, the sales response of segment s is likely to increase either with continuously diminishing returns (downward concave) or with increasing and then decreasing returns (S-shaped). These non-linearities are introduced in the sales response function $q(y_{st})$. The functional form used in this Media Aid module of the ADSTRAT system deviates from the MEDIAC model and, instead, follows that specified in the ADBUDG model[16] and discussed in Chapter 5:[17]

$$q(y_{st}) = \min + (\max - \min)\frac{y_{st}^{\sigma}}{\phi + y_{st}^{\sigma}} \tag{7.4}$$

where:

$q(y_{st})$ = the average percentage of sales potential in market segment s at time t realized with an exposure value level of y_{st},

$\min$ = the minimum average percentage of sales without any advertising,

$\max$ = the maximum average percentage of sales with an infinite number of insertions (i.e., saturation advertising),

---

Figure 7.15

Editing the Media Aid Option (Screen #1)

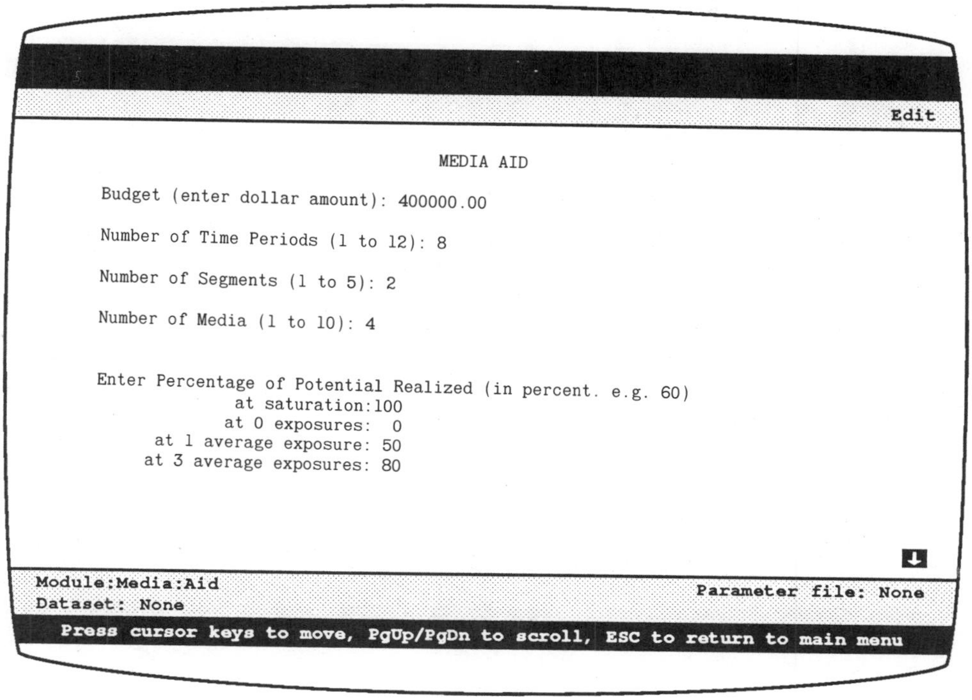

```
                                                                    Edit

                            MEDIA AID
      Budget (enter dollar amount): 400000.00

      Number of Time Periods (1 to 12): 8

      Number of Segments (1 to 5): 2

      Number of Media (1 to 10): 4


      Enter Percentage of Potential Realized (in percent. e.g. 60)
                    at saturation:100
                    at 0 exposures:  0
              at 1 average exposure: 50
              at 3 average exposures: 80




Module:Media:Aid                                    Parameter file: None
Dataset: None
  Press cursor keys to move, PgUp/PgDn to scroll, ESC to return to main menu
```

ϕ, σ = parameters that describes the sensitivity of the segment to advertising.

The term $q(y_{st})$ can be thought of as the probability that an individual in segment s with an exposure value of y would purchase the advertised brand in period t. If we know how much a segment member would typically spend on the product during period t, and the number of people in segment s, then we can represent total sales in segment s at time t as:

$$S_{st} = N_s m_{st} q(y_{st}) \qquad (7.5)$$

where:

S_{st} = sales in segment s at time t,

N_s = population size (number of individuals) in segment s,

m_{st} = average sales potential per person in segment s at time t.

These four equations (7.2–7.5) are sufficient to compute the sales that can be derived from a given schedule. By entering values for each of the parameters, the user can simulate consumer response to various schedules of insertions. However, *a priori*, the manager might not have a clear idea of what would be a "good"

─────────────── Figure 7.16 ───────────────

Editing the Media Aid Option (Screen #2)

```
                                                              Edit
                                                                ⬆

    Population (Number of Consumers) and
    Potential (Average Dollar Sales per Consumer) in each Segment
    Segment       1         2         3         4         5

    Population: 45000.00: 50000.00:_____:_____:_____
    Potential :     3.00:     7.50:_____:_____:_____

    Memory Constant (e.g. 0.75):0.70

    Exposure Values (Source Effect) and
    Probability of Exposure (Probability of seeing ad in vehicle)
    Media        1   2   3   4   5   9   7   8   9   10

    Exposure
      Value   :1.50:1.25:0.75:0.50:____:____:____:____:____:____
    Exposure
    Prob.     :0.40:0.40:0.50:0.30:____:____:____:____:____:____
                                                                ⬇

    Module:Media:Aid                          Parameter file: None
    Dataset: None
    Press cursor keys to move, PgUp/PgDn to scroll, ESC to return to main menu
```

schedule, and probably does not have the time (or patience) to evaluate all possible alternatives. Therefore, a heuristic procedure can be applied to systematically search through the possibilities to identify the insertion schedule that produces the highest level of sales within a certain budget constraint. These two options will be discussed in the following sections.

Selecting the MediaAid Option

The media aid module is accessed by selecting "Module" from the main menu, and then selecting "Media" and "MediaAid." The system displays the first screen of the input template (Figure 7.14). To enter information about the brand, media, and consumer segments, the user should select "Edit" from the main menu, and the cursor will move to the template area.

Defining Model Parameters

The media aid template consists of seven input screens. Figures 7.15 to 7.21 display these pages, and provide an example of the parameters described in this section. Unless otherwise noted, parameter values *must* be entered for each period, segment, and media option included in the analysis.

─────────── **Figure 7.17** ───────────

Editing the Media Aid Option (Screen #3)

```
                                                              Edit
                                                               ⬆

   Effective reach
   (Percentage of Audience that belongs to Segment, e.g. 16.0)
   Segments   1     2     3     4     5
   Media
       1   : 0.75:10.00:_____:_____:_____
       2   :14.00:11.25:_____:_____:_____
       3   :30.00:20.00:_____:_____:_____
       4   : 1.80:34.00:_____:_____:_____
       5   :_____:_____:_____:_____:_____
       9   :_____:_____:_____:_____:_____
       7   :_____:_____:_____:_____:_____
       8   :_____:_____:_____:_____:_____
       9   :_____:_____:_____:_____:_____
      10   :_____:_____:_____:_____:_____



                                                               ⬇
   Module:Media:Aid                          Parameter file: None
   Dataset: None
   Press cursor keys to move, PgUp/PgDn to scroll, ESC to return to main menu
```

Budget. The user first enters the size of the advertising budget to allocate. This value should be derived from the budgeting analyses discussed earlier. The media aid model will recommend how this investment should be allocated over time and media options. In the example shown in Figure 7.15, the value of $4,000,000 is entered.

As discussed in Chapter 5, the advertising budget depends, in part, on media costs and the efficiency of the media plan. Therefore, the user might develop the budget and media plan through an iterative process of testing and refinement. A tentative budget could first be defined following the recommendations and evaluations obtained in the budgeting module. Then, this information would be entered into the media aid module, where the user can evaluate how changes in the budget would affect the estimated media schedule and sales. If the two procedures produce different sales estimates, then the user can fine tune the parameters of each method to produce results that are internally consistent and externally supported.

Number of Time Periods. Next, the user indicates the number of time periods to be analyzed. The media analysis can be conducted over a maximum of twelve periods. Typically, the media plan is annual and periods are defined as months.

—————————————— Figure 7.18 ——————————————

Derivation of an Estimate of the Effective Reach Measures

Media Vehicle
Readership

	No	Yes
Female		n_3
Male	n_1	n_2

Segmenting
Variable

Individuals
in Segment

Individuals
in Audience

However, the media plan could be developed on a quarterly basis, where periods are used to represent weeks. This level of analysis allows the decision maker to study timing issues in greater detail. The user should note that some of the parameters of the media aid module depend on the definition of period length. For example, the memory constant (Figure 7.16) represents the percentage of exposure value recalled from one period to the next. This constant would increase as the period length is reduced.

Number of Segments. The number of segments corresponds to the number of target markets. Given that various segments have different media habits, sizes, and sales potential, it is appropriate to develop the media plan simultaneously for all market segments. The user can enter information on a maximum of five segments.

Number of Media. Ideally, all media would be included in the planning analysis. However, the data requirements become too burdensome when evaluating a large number of alternatives. In addition, as the number of options goes up, the computer execution time increases. When the user tests a small set of options, the computer can provide the rapid feedback necessary for performing multiple sensitivity analyses. Therefore, the user should enter information for those vehicles that he or she suspects will be cost effective based on earlier analyses. Up to ten media options can be evaluated with this module. The numbering of these options is arbitrary, but the numbers must be used consistently for all input of media information.

Response Function. The next set of questions asks the user to estimate the audience's purchase response to various advertising conditions (Figure 7.15). These judgments would typically be based on the manager's experience with marketing the product, advertising effectiveness research, and copy testing results. The parameters of the response function are derived from the user's answers to four questions: What is the percentage of the market potential realized

—————— Figure 7.19 ——————

Editing the Media Aid Option (Screen #4)

Media #	Average Cost Per Insertion Cost (in dollars)	Maximum Insertions per period	Audience size
1	:30000.00	: 1	: 60000.00
2	:45000.00	: 1	: 80000.00
3	:26000.00	: 1	: 30000.00
4	:10000.00	: 1	: 25000.00
5	:_____	:___	:_____
9	:_____	:___	:_____
7	:_____	:___	:_____
8	:_____	:___	:_____
9	:_____	:___	:_____
10	:_____	:___	:_____

Module:Media:Aid
Dataset: None   Parameter file: None
Press cursor keys to move, PgUp/PgDn to scroll, ESC to return to main menu

(a) at saturation levels of advertising, (b) with zero advertising exposures, (c) with one ad exposure, and (d) with three ad exposures? These values should be entered as percentage points (e.g., 20 for 20 percent).

One way to think about market potential is as the probability that people will buy the advertised brand given that they are purchasing a product in the category. From this perspective, the market potential values can be treated as market share estimates under alternative advertising scenarios. The segment sales potential (Figure 7.16) would then be defined as the average category expenditures by a segment member during one time period. The user can test how the level of competition might affect the sales and scheduling results by varying the response function estimates to represent different levels of competition.

Alternatively, the decision maker can scale the market potential values from 0 to 100 percent, where 100 percent represents an average segment member's purchase behavior under saturation advertising (as shown in the example in Figure 7.15). In this case, the sales potential values (Figure 7.16) are expressed as the amount an individual in segment s would spend on the advertised brand during one time period with saturation advertising. The second option permits the user to define the response function with a greater degree of precision

Figure 7.20

Editing the Media Aid Option (Screen #5)

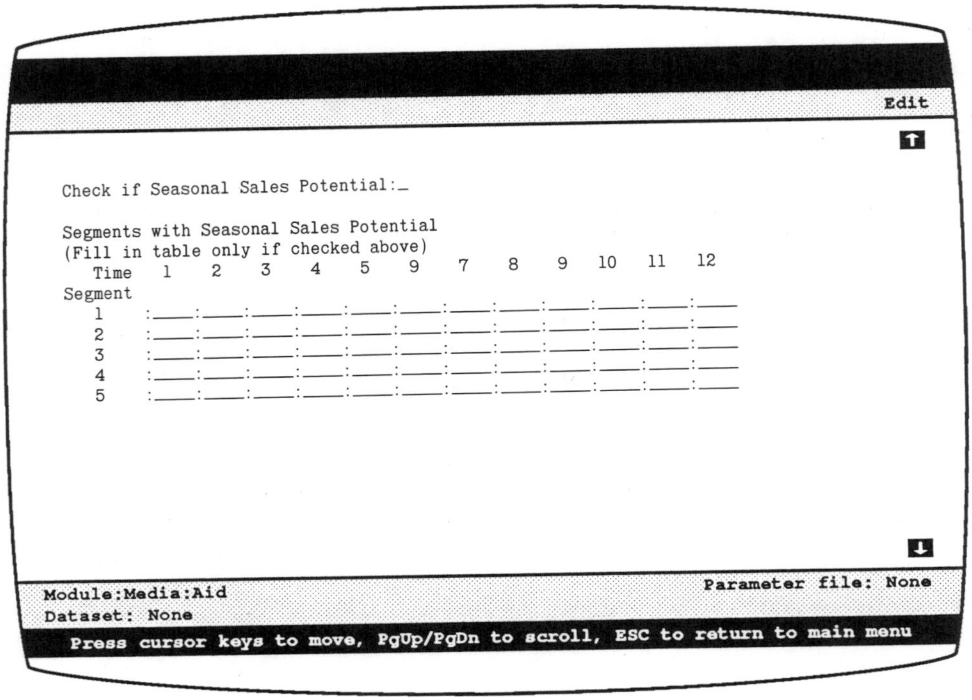

(particularly when market share values are small). The reader should note, however, that the choice between these two alternatives is somewhat arbitrary, since the curvature, and not the range, of the response function determines the model's selection of a particular media schedule.

Population by Segment. On the next page of the template (Figure 7.16), the user first enters the number of individuals or households that correspond to potential customers in a given segment.

Potential by Segment. The system then asks the user to indicate how much money consumers in each segment might spend on the product or brand during one time period. As discussed above, the appropriate answer depends on the definition of market coverage. If market share estimates were entered, then the user should input the total average expenditures per capita in this segment for the entire product category. If instead, the user entered information on the brand's purchase likelihood, then the potential sales figures should be expressed in terms of the average amount spent on the brand with saturation advertising. In the example in Figure 7.16, the user has specified that members of Segment 1 would purchase $3.00 of the brand per period with saturation advertising.

Figure 7.21

Editing the Media Aid Option (Screen #6)

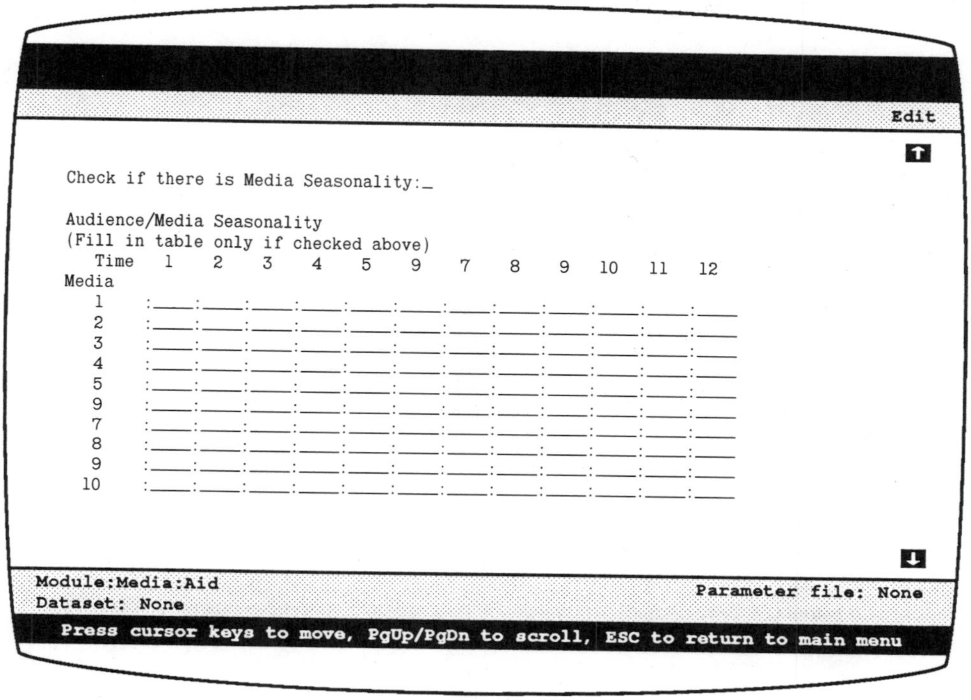

```
                                                                    Edit
                                                                     ⬆

   Check if there is Media Seasonality:_

   Audience/Media Seasonality
   (Fill in table only if checked above)
       Time  1   2   3   4   5   9   7   8   9   10  11  12
   Media
       1   :____:____:____:____:____:____:____:____:____:____:____:____
       2   :____:____:____:____:____:____:____:____:____:____:____:____
       3   :____:____:____:____:____:____:____:____:____:____:____:____
       4   :____:____:____:____:____:____:____:____:____:____:____:____
       5   :____:____:____:____:____:____:____:____:____:____:____:____
       9   :____:____:____:____:____:____:____:____:____:____:____:____
       7   :____:____:____:____:____:____:____:____:____:____:____:____
       8   :____:____:____:____:____:____:____:____:____:____:____:____
       9   :____:____:____:____:____:____:____:____:____:____:____:____
       10  :____:____:____:____:____:____:____:____:____:____:____:____

                                                                     ⬇

   Module:Media:Aid                              Parameter file: None
   Dataset: None
   Press cursor keys to move, PgUp/PgDn to scroll, ESC to return to main menu
```

Memory Constant. The memory constant represents the percentage of the weighted exposure value which is retained from one period to the next. Some studies indicate that the forgetting rate might be between 10 and 25 percent per week, so the memory constant would be specified as 0.90 or 0.75, respectively. Of course this rate depends on a number of factors, including the complexity of the brand, the level of competition, the degree of audience involvement, the distinctiveness of the ad execution, etc. Ideally, the estimate of the memory constant will be based on copy testing research on the specific brand, ad campaign, and audience at hand.

It is important to note that this model assumes that the exposure value at the beginning of the media planning period is zero. This would be appropriate for new brands. However, if the user is developing a media plan for an existing, advertised brand, then he or she should create an artificial first period with an advertising rate corresponding to past advertising levels.

Media Option Source Effect. As defined earlier, these parameters represent the impact of the message in various media options, given that the audience is exposed to the advertisement. An index value of 1.00 indicates an average level of impact or message fit.

--- Figure 7.22 ---

Editing the Media Aid Option (Screen #7)

```
                                                                      Edit
                                                                       ⬆

   Check to estimate sales from Media Insertion Plan below: x
   (Otherwise, optimal insertion plan will be derived)

   Media Insertion Plan
   (Fill in table only if checked above)
      Time  1    2    3    4    5    9    7    8    9   10   11   12
   Media
      1   :  1:   0:   0:   0:   0:   0:   0:   0:___:___:___:____
      2   :  1:   0:   0:   0:   0:   1:   0:   0:___:___:___:____
      3   :  1:   1:   1:   1:   1:   1:   1:   0:___:___:___:____
      4   :  1:   1:   1:   1:   1:   1:   1:   1:___:___:___:____
      5   :___:___:___:___:___:___:___:___:___:___:___:____
      9   :___:___:___:___:___:___:___:___:___:___:___:____
      7   :___:___:___:___:___:___:___:___:___:___:___:____
      8   :___:___:___:___:___:___:___:___:___:___:___:____
      9   :___:___:___:___:___:___:___:___:___:___:___:____
     10   :___:___:___:___:___:___:___:___:___:___:___:____


   Module:Media:Aid                              Parameter file: None
   Dataset: None
   Press cursor keys to move, PgUp/PgDn to scroll, ESC to return to main menu
```

Exposure Probability. The user then enters information on ad exposure probability for each media option, scaled from 0.00 to 1.00. As previously described, these figures indicate the level of audience interest in the media option. If, for example, the audience of a particular television show paid attention to half of the commercials, then the exposure probability for this vehicle would be 0.50. Estimates of these values can be obtained through advertising research.

Effective Reach. On the next screen (Figure 7.17), effective reach data must be entered for each media option and segment in the analysis. Information on effective reach can be obtained through analyses of the survey dataset (as described in the section on media allocation). Let us take, for example, a case where an advertiser is targeting men, age 18 and over, and is considering advertising in a particular magazine. ADSTRAT's survey dataset contains information on consumers' characteristics and media habits. The user can crosstabulate the sex and magazine readership variables to produce a table like the one displayed in Figure 7.18. In this example, n_1 represents the number of individuals who belong to the target segment but are not in the audience (male nonreaders), while n_2 is the number of individuals in the segment that are also in the audience

---
— Figure 7.23 —

Example Output of Media Aid Option in Simulation Mode (Screen #1)

MainMenu	SaveOutput	PrintOutput		

Return to main menu and redisplay module parameters

Output

MEDIA AID

Sales per segment

Period	Segments 1	2	Total Sales	Expenses
1	16265.93	51355.10	67621.03	111000.00
2	17521.39	51535.49	69056.88	36000.00
3	18397.13	51661.73	70058.86	36000.00
4	19008.31	51750.09	70758.40	36000.00
5	19435.15	51811.93	71247.07	36000.00
9	30065.67	73005.48	103071.15	81000.00
7	27255.16	66806.30	94061.46	36000.00
8	18878.95	51690.37	70569.32	10000.00

Total Overall Sales: 616444.18
Ratio Cost/Budget: 0.955000

Module:Media:MediaAid   Parameter file: None
Dataset: None

Press cursor keys and PgUp/PgDn to scroll, ESC to return to main menu

(male readers). The number of individuals in the audience but not in the segment of interest is n_3 (female readers). The total audience size in the sample is simply $n_2 + n_3$. The effective reach measure can be computed as $n_2/(n_2 + n_3)$). Of course, other variables can be used for segmentation purposes, such as cluster membership or Sonite ownership.

Average Cost per Insertion. The system requests information on the ad insertion costs for each of the selected media options (Figure 7.19). This information can be obtained from the media dataset by running the media efficiency module described earlier. The user can also acquire cost figures on media alternatives that are not covered in ADSTRAT's database (e.g., outdoor advertising), and enter them into the system.

Maximum Number of Insertions. Next, the user inputs the maximum number of insertions for each media option. As noted earlier, there may be constraints on the number of ads that can appear in an option during a particular time period. If, for example, the media options were weekly publications (52 issues per year) and the media plan was being developed over four quarters, then the user would enter a value of 13 for each option.

──────────── Figure 7.24 ────────────

Example Output of Media Aid Option in Simulation Mode (Screen #2)

```
 MainMenu          SaveOutput        PrintOutput
 Return to main menu and redisplay module parameters
                                                              Output
                                                                  ⬆

        MEDIA AID Schedule

        Media--Time   1   2   3   4   5   9   7   8

            1         1   0   0   0   0   0   0   0
            2         1   0   0   0   0   1   0   0
            3         1   1   1   1   1   1   1   0
            4         1   1   1   1   1   1   1   1




 Module:Media:MediaAid                          Parameter file: None
 Dataset: None
        Press cursor keys and PgUp/PgDn to scroll, ESC to return to main menu
```

Audience Size. The audience size is the average number of individuals who are exposed to the media vehicle. The user can acquire this information from the media dataset by executing the media efficiency module.

Segments with Seasonal Sales Potential. If the sales of the product fluctuate across periods, the user can check the box at the top of the next screen (Figure 7.20) and enter index values for the segments and time periods in the analysis. For example, sales of cold medicines increase in the winter, although this effect is less pronounced in warmer geographic regions. To reflect this, the user would enter a wider range of values for segments located in colder regions. An index value of 1.00 indicates average sales in a particular period. If there is no seasonality, this table can be left blank and the system assumes a default value of 1.00 for each period.

Media Seasonality. The audience sizes of the various media options may also fluctuate across time periods (Figure 7.21). If there is media seasonality, the user should check the box at the top of the screen and fill in data for the appropriate media options and time periods. An index value of 1.00 indicates an average audience size, a value greater than 1.00 indicates a relatively large audience, and

---

Figure 7.25

Editing the Media Aid Option for Optimization Mode

```
                                                              Edit
                                                               ↑

    Check to estimate sales from Media Insertion Plan below:_
    (Otherwise, optimal insertion plan will be derived)

    Media Insertion Plan
    (Fill in table only if checked above)
     Time   1    2    3    4    5    9    7    8    9   10   11   12
    Media
      1   :  1:   0:   0:   0:   0:   0:   0:   0:____:____:____:____
      2   :  1:   0:   0:   0:   0:   1:   0:   0:____:____:____:____
      3   :  1:   1:   1:   1:   1:   1:   1:   0:____:____:____:____
      4   :  1:   1:   1:   1:   1:   1:   1:   1:____:____:____:____
      5   :____:____:____:____:____:____:____:____:____:____:____:____
      9   :____:____:____:____:____:____:____:____:____:____:____:____
      7   :____:____:____:____:____:____:____:____:____:____:____:____
      8   :____:____:____:____:____:____:____:____:____:____:____:____
      9   :____:____:____:____:____:____:____:____:____:____:____:____
     10   :____:____:____:____:____:____:____:____:____:____:____:____


    Module:Media:Aid                              Parameter file: None
    Dataset: None
    Press cursor keys to move, PgUp/PgDn to scroll, ESC to return to main menu
```

---

a value less than 1.00 describes a smaller than average audience. For example, an index of 1.20 indicates that the audience size in that period is 20 percent higher than during a regular period.

Optimal Insertion Plan. On the last screen of the input template (Figure 7.22), the user chooses whether the media aid module will estimate the optimal schedule of ad insertions or simulate the market's response to a user-specified media plan. If the box at the top of the screen is not checked, then the system will search for the schedule that will produce the largest total sales over the planning period, subject to the constraints on ad budget and numbers of insertions per period.[18]

Media Insertion Plan. If the box at the top of the screen is checked, then the user must enter a schedule of ad insertions in the matrix that appears below. The decision maker specifies the placement of ads in media options and time periods by entering the desired number of insertions in each of the corresponding fields. These values can be any positive integer, but there is no guarantee that the plan will conform to the constraints specified earlier. As shown in the example in Figure 7.22, the user has asked the system to predict the performance of a media plan which places the greatest weight on options 3 and 4.

--- **Figure 7.26** ---

Example Output of Media Aid Option in Optimization Mode (Screen #1)

```
 MainMenu        SaveOutput        PrintOutput
 Return to main menu and redisplay module parameters
                                                               Output


                           MEDIA AID

      Sales per segment

                 Segments
      Period      1        2       Total Sales      Expenses
      ------    --------  --------  -----------     ---------
        1       16265.93  51355.10    67621.03      111000.00
        2       28015.15  72701.39   100716.54       81000.00
        3       35585.39  86892.92   122478.31       81000.00
        4       40401.37  90991.13   131392.50       71000.00
        5       38381.36  84100.10   122481.45       45000.00
        9       27282.35  58364.41    85646.76           0.00
        7       18769.42  39436.52    58205.94           0.00
        8       12602.02  26140.28    38742.30           0.00

      Total Overall Sales: 727284.83
      Ratio Cost/Budget: 0.972500
                                                                  ⬇

 Module:Media:MediaAid                        Parameter file: None
 Dataset: None
      Press cursor keys and PgUp/PgDn to scroll, ESC to return to main menu
```

The Media Aid Output

Figures 7.23 and 7.24 show the two screens of output corresponding to the schedule specified in Figure 7.22 (simulation mode). On the first page, the system displays the estimated sales for each segment and time period, and the total sales over the entire planning period. The module also reports the advertising expenses for this media plan.[19]

If the optimization option is chosen (as shown in Figure 7.25), the output presents the sales results for the "optimal" schedule (Figures 7.26 and 7.27). Recall that, in this example, the user specified the maximum number of insertions per media option per period as one (Figure 7.19). Therefore, the system determines whether or not to place a single ad in a given media option in a given period. The scheduling recommendations are shown on the second page of output (Figure 7.27).

Comparing the results of the simulation and optimization runs, the model was able to produce an almost 20 percent higher level of predicted sales than the user-supplied schedule with an equivalent budget. As described in the introduction, the user must now reflect on these results and evaluate whether they are consistent with his or her knowledge of the market. The sales differences appear

─────────── Figure 7.27 ───────────

Example Output of Media Aid Option in Optimization Mode (Screen #2)

```
 MainMenu        SaveOutput        PrintOutput
 Return to main menu and redisplay module parameters

                                                      Output
                                                        ⬆

     Optimal MEDIA AID Schedule

     Media--Time   1   2   3   4   5   9   7   8

          1        1   0   0   0   0   0   0   0
          2        1   1   1   1   1   0   0   0
          3        1   1   1   1   0   0   0   0
          4        1   1   1   0   0   0   0   0




 Module:Media:MediaAid                    Parameter file: None
 Dataset: None
      Press cursor keys and PgUp/PgDn to scroll, ESC to return to main menu
```

to be due to the heavy initial advertising in the second analysis. This scheduling is, in part, a consequence of the model's assumption that the initial exposure value in each segment is zero. This situation corresponds to a new brand introduction campaign, but would not be realistic for an existing brand. In the latter case, the user may want to insert some number of control periods at the beginning of the analysis to represent past advertising practices. The user should also consider the "end effects" discussed in the context of the budget aid module (Chapter 5). The model does not consider the carryover effects of advertising past the last planning period. To minimize this problem, the user can specify a greater number of periods than the actual media planning period.

Conclusion ───

In this chapter, we have presented various methods that can provide the advertiser with insights on how to allocate the advertising budget across media vehicle options. We started with simple cost per thousand calculations and then progressed to more sophisticated and complex model-based approaches. It is suggested that the user start with elementary analyses of a broad range of alternatives and then move to a more detailed analysis of a select group of media options. ADSTRAT facilitates this process by allowing the user to easily move between modules and conduct sensitivity analyses on model parameters.

References

1. For a review of consumer information processing issues associated with media class selection, see Rossiter, John R. and Larry Percy (1987), *Advertising and Promotion Management*, New York: McGraw-Hill, Chapter 15.
2. Engel, James F. and Martin R. Warshaw (1964), "Allocating Advertising Dollars by Linear Programming," *Journal of Advertising Research*, 42–48.
3. Little, John D. C. and Leonard M. Lodish (1969), "A Media Planning Calculus," *Operations Research*, 17 (January–February), 1–35.
4. The media dataset which accompanies ADSTRAT is consistent with audience size information published by Simmons Market Research Bureau, Inc., New York, and rate information reported by the Standard Rate & Data Service, Wilmett, IL. See Chapter 2 for additional details.
5. The screen displays the abbreviated names of the media vehicles. The full names are listed in Table 2.6 of Chapter 2.
6. For a more detailed discussion of media planning models, see Rust, Roland T. (1986), *Advertising Media Models*, Lexington, MA: Lexington Books.
7. Engel, James F. and Martin R. Warshaw (1964), *opus cited*.
8. Internal overlap is generally higher than external overlap. Therefore, advertisers will often advertise in different communication outlets if the goal is to build reach, and advertise in the same vehicles if the intention is to increase frequency.
9. For print media, the survey measured people's readership of general classes of alternatives (e.g., fashion magazines), rather than specific vehicles (*Bazaar, Glamour*). These figures can be used to adjust reach figures across classes, but it is not possible to precisely estimate the effective reach of individual vehicles. For planning purposes, the user can assume that vehicles within the same class have equal reach.
10. Note that the index values shown in Figures 7.9 and 7.11 are used for illustration purposes, and do not represent the actual reach and effectiveness of the options.
11. Better estimates of these values can be obtained experimentally by testing an advertisement's performance in alternative vehicles and options.
12. For example, in Figures 7.10 and 7.12, the dramatic difference in effective exposures (78,239,000 versus 28,801,000) is primarily due to the use of default index values in the first case, rather than to differences in schedule effectiveness.
13. Simon, Julian L. and Johan L. Arndt (1980), "The Shape of the Advertising Response Function," *Journal of Advertising Research*, 20 (August), 11–28.
14. The notation in this section follows the presentation of the model in Little, John D. C. and Leonard Lodish (1966), "A Media Selection Model and its Optimization by Dynamic Programming," *Industrial Management Review*, 8 (Fall), 15–23. ADSTRAT's implementation of the MEDIAC model does not explicitly consider audience duplication across vehicles. For a discussion of the duplication issue and a description of MEDIAC's pairwise duplication estimation procedure, the reader should consult Little, John D. C. and Leonard Lodish (1969), *opus cited*.
15. Little, John D. C. (1970), "Models and Managers: The Concept of a Decision Calculus," *Management Science*, 16 (April), B466–485.

16. Little, John D. C. (1970), *opus cited*.
17. This response function is particularly attractive because it is very flexible and its parameters can be easily assessed from managers' subjective judgments.
18. In this case, information in the scheduling matrix is ignored.
19. The schedule shown in Figure 7.24 is just a copy of the input information.

APPENDIX

Using the ADSTRAT System

The ADSTRAT system has been designed to run on any IBM-compatible personal computer operating under the PC DOS or MS-DOS operating system.[1] The minimum hardware necessary for running ADSTRAT is a computer with at least one 3½″ disk drive or two 5¼″ disk drives. If you will be installing ADSTRAT on a hard disk, then only one disk drive (of either type) is required. If you have a 3½″ disk drive, all of the ADSTRAT files will be on a single diskette supplied with the manual. If you are using 5¼″ diskettes, two diskettes are supplied with the manual. One of the diskettes is the program disk and the other is the data disk. Although a hard disk and/or math coprocessor will speed up ADSTRAT's operation, they are not required.

ADSTRAT's user interface has been designed to be convenient and easy to learn. In this Appendix, we describe how to install the software on your computer, discuss the use of the keyboard and the format of the display screen, and explain ADSTRAT's menu options and functions. The focus of this Appendix will be on the general functions of the user interface (e.g., loading, saving, and printing files). The operation of specific analysis modules is discussed in the corresponding chapters of this manual.

System Installation

Installing ADSTRAT involves the following steps:

1. Boot Your Computer
2. Make a Working Copy of ADSTRAT
3. Install the ANSI.SYS Driver
4. Start ADSTRAT
5. Test Your Printer
6. Exit ADSTRAT

We now discuss each of these steps in turn.

STEP 1. Boot Your Computer

Your computer and the operating system (PC DOS or MS-DOS) must be running before you can install or run ADSTRAT. After switching on the computer, the monitor may ask for the date and time, and will then display the DOS prompt ("A>," "B>," "C>," etc., depending on your computer configuration). Because of the variety of possible configurations, we will use the symbol ">" to indicate the DOS prompt. Unless otherwise noted, you should press the "Enter" key (also labeled "Return") after each of the DOS commands listed in this section.

STEP 2. Make a Working Copy of ADSTRAT

The ADSTRAT software is not copy protected and you are permitted to make one working copy of the software and store the original diskette(s) for backup purposes. You are licensed to use this software for your own use, but may not sell or transfer reproductions of the software or manual to other parties in any way, nor rent or lease the software to others. You may use one copy of the software on a single computer. You may not network the product or otherwise use it on more than one computer or computer terminal at the same time.

If your computer has a hard disk, we recommend that you install the ADSTRAT software on the hard disk to speed the software's operation. If not, then we suggest that you make a working copy of the original (master) diskette(s) which accompany this manual.

If you install ADSTRAT on your hard disk: First create a directory on the hard disk to store the ADSTRAT files. If you are in a subdirectory, switch to the main directory by typing "cd\" at the DOS prompt. Then, create the ADSTRAT directory by typing:

```
> md adstrat
```

Move into this new directory by typing:

```
> cd adstrat
```

Now, you can copy the ADSTRAT files from the master diskette(s) supplied with this manual onto your hard disk.

If you have a 3½" diskette: Insert your ADSTRAT master disk in drive A. (If your 3½" disk drive is different from drive A, please substitute the appropriate drive letter for "a".) Then type:

```
> copy a:*.*
```

Your ADSTRAT software is now loaded on your hard disk and you can skip to step 3 (Installing the ANSI.SYS Driver). Store the ADSTRAT master diskette in a safe location.

If you have 5¼" diskettes: Insert your ADSTRAT master program disk in drive A. (If your 5¼" disk drive is different from drive A, please substitute the appropriate drive letter for "a".) Then type:

```
> copy a:*.*
```

Remove your ADSTRAT master program disk from the drive and insert your ADSTRAT master data disk. Then type:

```
> copy a:*.*
```

Your ADSTRAT software is now loaded on your hard disk and you can skip to Step 3 (installing the ANSI.SYS driver). Store the ADSTRAT master diskettes in a safe location.

If you do not have a hard disk: Although you could run ADSTRAT directly from the master diskette(s) supplied with this manual, it is safer to use a working copy of the software. You can make a working copy with a two disk drive computer system by executing the following instructions:

■ Insert a blank diskette in drive B:

■ Insert your DOS diskette containing the DOS FORMAT command in drive A and move to that drive by typing:

```
> a:
```

■ Format the new diskette by typing:

```
A> format b:
```

■ Remove the DOS diskette from drive A.

If you are using 5¼" diskettes, you will need to repeat this formatting operation for a second diskette. One diskette will be used to create a program disk and another will be used to create a data disk.

■ Insert the ADSTRAT master diskette into drive A.

■ Copy the ADSTRAT files by typing:

```
A> copy a:*.* b:
```

If you are using 5¼" diskettes, you will need to repeat this copy operation for both the program diskette and the data diskette.

You can now store the ADSTRAT master diskette(s) in a safe location and use the working copy to run the ADSTRAT system. Note that the DOS operating system is not stored on the ADSTRAT diskette. Therefore, you cannot boot your computer directly from this diskette. You must first boot your system with the proper DOS diskette in drive A, wait for the "A>" prompt, and then insert the ADSTRAT diskette(s).

STEP 3. Install the ANSI.SYS Driver

ADSTRAT requires that the ANSI.SYS device driver be loaded in memory before executing the program. ANSI.SYS provides enhanced screen and keyboard functions which are used by the ADSTRAT program. To install ANSI.SYS, first check to see if this file is present in the root directory of your boot diskette or hard disk. If not, then copy the file named ANSI.SYS from your original DOS diskette to this location. Next, create a file named CONFIG.SYS (or edit the existing CONFIG.SYS file) in the root directory, and include the command DEVICE=ANSI.SYS. This command causes the operating system to replace the standard input and output support with the extended functions. Finally, load the driver in memory by rebooting the computer (press the [Ctrl], [Alt], and [Del] keys simultaneously). For more information about device drivers and system configuration, please consult your operating system manual.

When the ANSI.SYS driver has been successfully installed and the ADSTRAT program is started, the computer will clear the screen and then display the green ADSTRAT banner. The user can then press any key to continue. If the driver is not correctly installed, then the system will print a series of control characters (e.g., "[0m[2J[H") along with a monochrome banner. In this case, press the "Escape" key (also labeled "Esc") to exit ADSTRAT, edit the CONFIG.SYS file to include the ANSI.SYS driver (as described above), and reboot the system.

STEP 4. Start ADSTRAT

To start ADSTRAT, you must first select the drive where the working copy of ADSTRAT is inserted, or select the directory on your hard disk which contains the ADSTRAT files.

If ADSTRAT is installed on your hard disk: Move to the ADSTRAT directory by typing:

```
> cd adstrat
```

and then start the ADSTRAT program by typing:

```
> adstrat
```

You should see the ADSTRAT logo on the screen. Press any key to obtain a menu bar of options. You can now go to step 5, and continue through the ADSTRAT system.

If ADSTRAT is not installed on a hard disk: The procedure for starting ADSTRAT depends on whether you are using a single 3½" diskette or two 5¼" diskettes.

If you have a 3½" disk drive: Insert your working copy of the ADSTRAT diskette into the 3½" disk drive. Move to the ADSTRAT diskette by typing the corresponding drive letter, for example:

```
> a:
```

and then start the ADSTRAT program by typing:

```
> adstrat
```

You should see the ADSTRAT logo on the screen. Press any key to obtain a menu bar of options. You can now go to Step 5, and continue through the ADSTRAT system.

If you have two 5¼" disk drives: Insert your working copy of the ADSTRAT program diskette into drive A and your working copy of the ADSTRAT data diskette into drive B. Move to the ADSTRAT program diskette by typing:

```
> a:
```

and then start the ADSTRAT program by typing:

```
> adstrat
```

You should see the ADSTRAT logo on the screen. Press any key to obtain the menu bar. Next, choose the utilities option by pressing the right arrow key once (the Utilities option is then highlighted) and press the "Enter" key. A new menu bar will be displayed at the top of the screen. Select the NewDatasetPath option by pressing the right arrow key until this option is highlighted and press "Enter." You can now enter the new path to the ADSTRAT files. If the program diskette is in drive B, then type b: at the prompt. You can save this information by pressing the "Enter" key. To exit the NewDatasetPath mode without saving your changes, press the "Escape" key (also labeled "Esc" on some computers).
   You can now continue through the ADSTRAT system.

STEP 5. Test Your Printer

The ADSTRAT system has been designed to work with any printer. It does not use any special print characters. To test your printer, first start the ADSTRAT program as described above and press a key to bypass the logo. The module menu bar appears.

- Press the "Enter" key to select the module menu.
- Press the right arrow key until the Budget option is highlighted and then press "Enter".

The screen will display the options for the Budget module.

- Press the right arrow key until the BudgetAid option is highlighted and press "Enter".

The BudgetAid module is loaded into memory and the corresponding template is displayed on your screen. The menu changes to the main menu bar.

- Press the right arrow key until the Utilities option is highlighted and press "Enter".
- Press the right arrow key until the PrintParameters option is highlighted.
- Check that your printer is turned on.
- Press the "Enter" key to start printing.

The menu returns to the main menu bar when printing is done.

STEP 6. Exit ADSTRAT

You can exit ADSTRAT by choosing the Quit option from the main menu bar. You can press the "Escape" key at any point in the ADSTRAT system to return to the main menu.

User Interface

In this section, we briefly describe ADSTRAT's use of the keyboard and the basic structure of the display screen.

--- **Figure A.1** ---

Cursor Keys

Home	Up Arrow	PageUp
Left Arrow		Right Arrow
End	Down Arrow	PageDn

or

Insert	Home	PageUp
Delete	End	PageDn

	Up Arrow	
Left Arrow	Down Arrow	Right Arrow

Special Keys

ADSTRAT uses a familiar menu bar and template format to minimize system learning time. Most of your interaction with ADSTRAT is through the standard alpha-numeric keys on the computer keyboard. The system does employ some special keys which require a short explanation. These keys are the cursor movement keys, the "Delete" key, and the "Escape" key. The cursor keys can be found on the right side of the keyboard, and are shown in Figure A.1.

The arrow keys. The arrow keys move the cursor across menu options or template fields. When a menu bar is displayed, you can highlight the various menu options by pressing the right and left arrow keys. In the edit mode, the arrow keys move the cursor from one data entry field to another. The cursor location is indicated by a blinking underscore. If the cursor is moved past the last input field on the screen, the program automatically displays the next page of the template.[2] Similarly, if you move the cursor past the first field, the system automatically displays the preceding page. When the system is showing the output of a module, the up and down arrow keys allow you to scroll through the results line by line.

The "Page Up" and "Page Down" keys. Whenever system input or output is displayed on the screen, you can page through the material by pressing the "Page Up" and "Page Down" keys. These keys are sometimes labeled "Pg Up" and "Pg Dn," respectively. The displayed information has embedded page breaks which correspond to logical sections of the input or output.

The "Home" and "End" keys. The "Home" key moves you to the beginning of the input or output. The "End" key displays the last page of this information.

The "Delete" key. The "Delete" key erases information in the template field at the current cursor location.

——————— Figure A.2 ———————

The ADSTRAT Screen

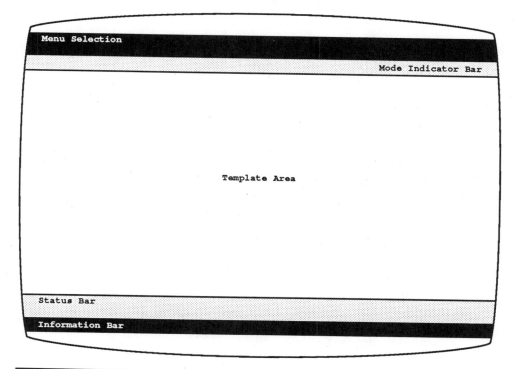

The "Escape" key. The "Escape" key returns you to the system's main menu. It is used to exit from ADSTRAT's edit mode, but can also be used to return from the system's other modes (e.g., Output, File, etc.).

The Display Screen

When you first start the program, the system displays the ADSTRAT logo and waits for you to press any key. It then displays the initial menu bar and allows you to select an analysis module. All of the analysis modules have basically the same screen format. The screen is composed of five parts (as shown in Figure A.2). The display is delimited by two reverse-video bars; one towards the top of the screen, which is called the "mode indicator bar," and one near the bottom, which we call the "status bar." We describe each of the five regions in turn.

Menu section. The menu section appears at the top of the screen. The first line displays the menu bar with its various options. The second line provides a brief description of the highlighted option. You can review the functions of the available options by moving the highlighted region across the alternatives. The second line is also used to enter file names or disk path information requested by the system, or to select file names from a list.

Mode indicator bar. The mode indicator bar displays the system's current mode of operation (on the far right side of the screen). For example, while you are editing the template parameters, the name "Edit" appears in this bar. Other names that might appear (as described below) are Main, Module, Output, File, and Utilities.

Template area. The template area is the largest portion of the ADSTRAT screen. When a module is loaded, the corresponding input template is displayed in this area. You are able to specify model parameters and select variables for analysis by editing information in the template (as described in Chapters 3 through 7). The template area is also used to display the output of ADSTRAT's analyses. This area can be thought of as a window into a larger region. You can scroll through this region by pressing the "Page Up" and "Page Down" keys, as described earlier.

Status bar. The status bar provides three pieces of information. On the first line, on the far left side of the screen, the system lists the name of the module that has been selected. As the choice of a module involves the selection of both an advertising decision and a specific type of analysis, both pieces of information appear. On the right-hand side of this line, the system displays the name of the current parameter file. When a module is first loaded, the label "None" appears. If the user loads or saves a set of module parameters, then the name of this file is displayed. On the second line of the status bar, on the left-hand side of the screen, the system displays the names of the data sets (separated by commas) that are accessed by the analysis module.

Information line. The information line appears at the bottom of the screen and provides two types of information. First, it gives instructions for interacting with the ADSTRAT software. For example, it can describe the use of the keyboard or suggest that you enter a file name. Its second function is to report the system's current activities. For example, when you first select a module, the system displays the message "Loading module." When a module is being executed, the system notes that it is "Loading data" and then reports the approximate percentage of the analysis which has been performed. When the analysis is completed, the output is displayed in the center of the screen. The information line also reports errors in variable selection or data input.

Moving Around ADSTRAT

ADSTRAT's functions are organized according to a hierarchical menu structure. The top-level menu is called the main menu. From this level, you can access ADSTRAT's modules, load, edit, and save module parameters, and display module output. To select an item from a menu, highlight the desired option using the right or left arrow key and then press "Enter." Alternatively, you can choose an option by pressing the first letter of the option's name.[3]

The Main Menu

The main menu lists the various software functions. When ADSTRAT is first started, the main menu presents an abbreviated list of alternatives (Module, Utilities, and Quit. Once a module has been selected, the system displays the full menu (Output, Module, Edit, File, Utilities, and Quit). The options are:

Output: Run the current module and display the results.

Module: Select a new module.

Edit: Move the cursor to the template area, and permit entry or editing of module parameters.

File: Load, save, or delete parameter files.

Utilities: Change the dataset path, print the template, or clear module parameters.

Quit: Exit the ADSTRAT system (after requesting confirmation.)

These options are described in more detail in the following section.

The Module Menu

The first step in using the ADSTRAT software is to pick an analysis module. When the Module option is selected from the main menu, the system displays five alternatives corresponding to the stages in the advertising planning process (situation analysis, objectives, budgeting, creative strategy, and media planning). After choosing one of these decisions, the system displays a new menu bar with a set of specific analysis tools (described in Chapters 3 through 7 of this manual). When you select an alternative from this list, the system loads the module and displays the corresponding template.

The Edit Mode

Once a module has been accessed, you can edit its parameters by selecting the Edit option. The cursor will move to the template area. When you are finished entering information, press "Escape" to return to the main menu.

The Output Menu

If you have entered the required information into the module template, you can then select Output to run the analysis. When the analysis is complete, the system displays the results and presents three menu options: MainMenu (return to the main menu), SaveOutput (save the output in a file), and PrintOutput (print the output). An example of the output from the media efficiency module is shown in Figure A.3. To print this information, turn on your printer and select PrintOutput. The actual printout is shown in Figure A.4. You can also save the output in a file for later inclusion in a report. Select the SaveOutput option, type in the desired file name, and press "Enter." The output will be saved to disk.

The File Menu

After entering information into a module template, you may want to save this input so that it can be retrieved, edited, and re-analyzed at a future time.

—————————————— Figure A.3 ——————————————

Example Output for Media Efficiency Option

```
MainMenu        SaveOutput        PrintOutput
Return to main menu and redisplay module parameters
                                                          Output
                                                            ⬆

                          MEDIA EFFICIENCY

   Vehicle Option    Audience Size    Cost/Insertion   Cost/Thousand
                        (000)             ($)              ($)
   ---------------   -------------    --------------   -------------
   CosmopoltnBW         2935             32170            10.96
   GoodHskpngBW         5142             66965            13.02
   LadiesHJrnBW         5121             52300            10.21
   McCallsBW            5275             51400             9.74
   ParentMgznBW         1729             29870            17.28
   RedbookBW            3891             43875            11.28
   SeventeenBW          1804             21100            11.70
   TrueStoryBW          1444             13355             9.25
   WomansDayBW          5632             53465             9.49

                                                            ⬇
   Module:Media:Efficiency                    Parameter file: None
   Dataset: media.dat
      Press cursor keys and PgUp/PgDn to scroll, ESC to return to main menu
```

These functions are provided in ADSTRAT's File menu. When the File option is selected from the main menu, the system displays the following alternatives: LoadParameters (load module parameters from disk file), SaveParameters (save module parameters to a disk file), DeleteFile (delete a parameter file from disk), NewFilePath (set new disk path to load/save/delete parameter files).

You can save the parameters for the current module by selecting the SaveParameters option. If there are no existing parameter files for this module, then ADSTRAT prompts you for a file name. If parameter files have already been saved on disk, the system displays their names in the menu section. You can select a file by pressing the arrow keys until the desired name is highlighted. Then press "Enter" to update (overwrite) the existing file. Alternatively, you can create a new file by pressing the "Escape" key and then entering its name at the prompt. The name of the parameter file is displayed in the status bar.

If you would like to retrieve a parameter file from disk, select the Load–Parameters option, and the system will provide you with a list of names corresponding to files that have been previously saved for this module. Use the arrow keys to highlight the desired file name and then press "Enter." The name of the parameter file is displayed in the status bar. Existing parameter files can also be

―――――――――――――――――― Figure A.4 ――――――――――――――――――

Example of Printer Output

```
Output from Module:Media:Efficiency      ADSTRAT, Version 1.0
Dataset: media.dat                       Copyright 1990
Fri Aug 03 15:08:45 1990                 H. Gatignon & R. Burke
```

MEDIA EFFICIENCY

Vehicle Option	Audience Size (000)	Cost/Insertion ($)	Cost/Thousand ($)
CosmopoltnBW	2935	32170	10.96
GoodHskpngBW	5142	66965	13.02
LadiesHJrnBW	5121	52300	10.21
McCallsBW	5275	51400	9.74
ParentMgznBW	1729	29870	17.28
RedbookBW	3891	43875	11.28
SeventeenBW	1804	21100	11.70
TrueStoryBW	1444	13355	9.25
WomansDayBW	5632	53465	9.49

deleted from disk by selecting DeleteFile, highlighting the file to be removed, and pressing "Enter".

The Utilities Menu

The Utilities menu provides four options: Information (display information about the ADSTRAT system), NewDatasetPath (set a new disk path to search for datasets), PrintParameters (print module parameters), and ClearParameters (clear module parameters and reset default values). The Information option prints a brief description of the ADSTRAT software. The NewDatasetPath option is used to configure ADSTRAT for operation on a computer with two 5¼" disk drives, where the program and data files are stored on two separate diskettes (as described earlier). The PrintParameters option prints the module template and its parameters. The ClearParameters option deletes the template input, allowing you to start on a new problem. (The template remains on the display screen, but all parameters are erased and replaced by the default values.)

Conclusion

The information in this Appendix will guide you through the ADSTRAT system and enable you to exploit its general capabilities. A detailed discussion of each of the analysis modules is presented in the body of the text. At this point, you should turn to Chapter 2 and begin developing an advertising plan with the assistance of ADSTRAT's models, methods, and datasets.

References

1. IBM and PC DOS are registered trademarks of International Business Machines, Corp. MS-DOS is a registered trademark of Microsoft Corp.

2. A template consists of a set of labeled fields for entering parameters or selecting variables for a specific analysis module. The information requirements of each template are described in Chapters 3 through 7.

3. If two menu options have names starting with the same letter, then the first option is selected by default. Use the cursor keys to select the second option.

INDEX